LETTERS
FROM
LOCKDOWN

LETTERS FROM LOCKDOWN

INTRODUCED BY

NATASHA KAPLINSKY

AND HER CHILDREN, ARLO AND KIKA

wren
&rook

First published in Great Britain in 2021 by Wren & Rook

Text copyright © Hodder & Stoughton Limited, 2021
Illustrations by Samuel Perrett, copyright © Hodder & Stoughton Limited, 2021
Design copyright © Hodder & Stoughton Limited, 2021
All rights reserved.

The moral rights of the authors and illustrator have been asserted.

The publisher will donate all profits, which will be a minimum of £1.50 for each
copy of the book sold, to Barnardo's.
Barnardo's is a charity registered in England and Wales with charity number 216250.

ISBN: 978 1526 36436 4
E-book ISBN: 978 1526 36455 5
10 9 8 7 6 5 4 3 2 1

MIX
Paper from
responsible sources
FSC
www.fsc.org   FSC® C104740

Wren & Rook
An imprint of
Hachette Children's Group
Part of Hodder & Stoughton
Carmelite House
50 Victoria Embankment
London EC4Y 0DZ

An Hachette UK Company
www.hachette.co.uk
www.hachettechildrens.co.uk

Printed and bound in Great Britain by Clays Ltd, Elcograf S.p.A

CONTENTS

Dear Reader,

Thank you for buying this book and for the time you will spend turning its pages.

I have always been a prolific letter writer and as news of the creeping virus was spreading fear around the globe and the Lockdowns began, I wanted to instil in our children the habit of letter writing as a way of reaching out to others; a habit that I hope will last them a lifetime. The joy of resorting to one of the oldest means of communication seemed too good to resist.

At first, our children, Arlo and Kika, were not convinced. At the ages of 12 and 11, their chief means of connecting with the outside world is electronic and instant. They took some persuading, but as a family we soon found pleasure in the gentle exchange of news with friends, neighbours, and distant family members. The arrival of the morning's post gave us something to look forward to amid the monotony of day-to-day Lockdown. We'd hope that amongst the grey bills and requests there might be a hand-written envelope: a reminder that although we were physically separated from those we loved, we were still connected by a piece of paper that had passed from their hands to ours.

Every letter received made us wonder how people elsewhere were passing these strange, challenging days. So many of our correspondents wrote of how they were using their time positively to help and support others. As Lockdown followed Lockdown, rather than writing to those we knew, we trawled the internet to find addresses of world leaders, film stars, musicians and sporting legends, and the everyday heroes whose stories we had read about in the news. Arlo and Kika had two questions: 'What were people doing with their time?' and 'How did they feel about the future?'

Like everyone else, we were fixated by the R-rate. We were shocked by the graphs and statistics that charted the daily advance of the virus – a virus that also made its way into our own home. Justin, my husband, was hit hard. The ambulance crew, in full PPE, gave us our first glimpse of the extraordinary dedication and kindness displayed by the NHS. As we dialled 999, we were acutely aware of the pressures on the system, and of the hardships that would follow. The aftershocks of the pandemic would be far-reaching and immeasurable.

As president of Barnardo's, I was being constantly updated on the worsening situation for children – those who were already most vulnerable. In its 155 year history, Barnardo's has supported children through two world wars and many other hardships, but the fight against the pandemic is today's challenge to overcome. Like other charities around the world, Barnardo's have suffered a huge drop in income at a time when its services are more in demand than ever. The pandemic has whipped up a perfect storm – increasing need while reducing resource. More children than ever are living in poverty, experiencing anxiety, and struggling with their mental health. More children are at risk of harm at home, online and in their communities.

As a family, we were determined to do something to help – and so came the idea of sharing these 'Letters From Lockdown'. Hachette generously agreed to support this anthology with all profits going to help support children left in the wake of COVID-19. We hope that this collection of letters will help to act as an emotional time capsule – distilling some sense of what happened behind the headlines in the year that everything changed. We are thrilled that our family project, beginning with a piece of paper, a pen and a stamp, has gone some way to help children who have paid a high price during the pandemic.

So what will you find as you turn these pages? To begin with, there is a version of the letter Arlo and Kika sent to every person in this book, together with early responses from some of our family. Their generous letters were the important starting point of this project. Then, grouped loosely by themes that stood out to us, you will hear from some incredible, beloved celebrities; inspiring frontline workers; and stay-at-home heroes who have all kindly shared their stories. It has been such fun connecting with so many wonderful people – only timing has stopped the adventure of reaching out to so many more.

Like us, I am sure that you will be touched by the range of experiences you'll read about – by the hardships and challenges, by the pivots and solutions that amazing people have come up with to help us all through Lockdown. We hope you will be endlessly inspired by the kindness and humanity that flow in abundance from the pages that follow.

As I write, here in the UK we are hoping for a safe end to restrictions. If all goes to plan, by the time you read this, let's hope that we will have travelled further towards more normal days when the words COVID and Coronavirus are a fading memory.

I dare to hope that one positive legacy of the pandemic will be the compassion and thoughtfulness shown by so many through those dark days. I also hope that our habit of sending letters will last far beyond Lockdown, and that you too are tempted to pick up a pen and write.

With my love and gratitude,

Natasha x

During Lockdown we are writing to a new person every day who has inspired us, to ask how Covid has affected their lives. We are hoping to publish a book called "Letters in Lockdown" and we are going to give all the money we raise to a charity helping people who have suffered during the Corona Virus.

We hope you don't mind that we are writing to you and that you will be happy to help us.

Our names are Arlo and Kika. We are brother and sister and we are 12 and 10 years old. We live on a farm in Sussex in England with lots of animals and have been home schooling and trying not to argue!

We are learning about lots of different things

and also about different people and what they have done in Lockdown. We would love to learn a bit about you and how you have been affected

How has your life changed what have you been doing to keep busy?

Do you feel positive about the futor? We don't know how we feel about it as it has been very hard not being able to see our friends and play in the way we used to.

Please write back to us. We will be checking the post every single day.
Thank you very very much.

Arlo and Kika.

A letter came in pink and blue
saying: tell us what it's like for you,
this Lockdown time which lasts an age
when all the world's a COVID stage
and with no friends or games to play
except online now every day
stuck at home, a sister and brother,
to take it out on one another?
'What's it like for you', you ask?
I'll try to settle to the task.

Well . . . sad – we miss you – a bit mad
and sometimes glad to slop about
in floppy clothes and not to rush
or be in a hurry or worry about doing this or that
but probably . . . just rather flat.

But then there's time to think and ponder,
to look about at all life's wonder.
Up above there's a cleaner sky
– no farting planes allowed to fly!
Should we all be asking why
and could this crisis now imply it's time to change our way of life
and how to seize each day and please the ones we love and think of
the other and know in your heart
you get if you give – it's the best way to live.

So is it time for a new start?

Lockdown will pass and we'll all move on
but its lovely now that your book will have shone
a light on how it was and what we thought
and what this COVID time has taught.

Your lives will have its lows and highs
but your futures, I hope, will be loving and wise.
Thank you darlings for your letter
May we learn from today so tomorrow is better.

Lots of love,
Yaya XX

This poem
is from our
mum's mum

Darling Arlo and Kika,

Thank you for your wonderful pink and blue letter.

So what did I do during Lockdown? Mmm, nothing, and it was really, really BORING.

Actually I didn't quite do nothing. I did a lot of thinking and here are some of the things on my mind.

I thought a lot about missing you, your cousins, your mum and dad and your uncle and aunt. Luckily, for some of the time in the summer, when the sun seemed to shine almost every day, we were able to visit each other in our gardens and that was fun. The dogs had a ball too!

But my thoughts weren't all full of fun. I remember when your dad was so badly struck down by COVID at the beginning of the pandemic. Ambulances were called a number of times and we were so worried about him. He was really sick for days and days and that must have been so hard for you. You and your mum also caught the virus but luckily it wasn't severe and we only knew about this after you had recovered. Just when we thought the worst was over, your other two grandparents became seriously ill with COVID just after Christmas. Poor Pa was especially ill and was rushed off to hospital by ambulance a number of times. He was really brave, but so too were the two of you. Your mum and dad were life savers and it was lucky that Pa was living next door.

One other thought has stayed with me right through this terrible time: none of us are safe until ALL of us are safe. We don't only wear masks to protect ourselves but also to protect others. As a development economist, I am particularly concerned about the poor, especially those living in developing economies. If we don't vaccinate the whole world, soon it will not only be a stain on our conscience, but it will also make us more vulnerable to new variants of the disease. That is also a lesson for life which doesn't only apply to COVID.

I've also thought about how grateful I am that our family has survived this pandemic when so many haven't. I'm happy the vaccine is being rolled out and for the difference this will make.

Now what we have to tackle urgently is climate crisis. This is something which Yaya and I, and all of our age group, have left you with. We are so sorry for that. But if enough people do enough of the right things then we might just do enough to save the planet for the generations to come.

Bravo for what you are doing now — and will no doubt do in the future. We love you both so deeply and want the best for you and for all the grandchildren in the world.

Remember the words of Nelson Mandela who was asked what 'ubuntu' means. He said it means that a person is only a person because they are part of a community. We need each other to be who we are and to flourish.

Lots of love,

Bops ⟵ *This is our mum's dad*

Dear Arlo and Kika,

Thank you for your letter. During Lockdown I have been going on lots of walks near the river.

We got a new pet who we named Albus. The dogs are a bit confused about what kind of dog Albus is. This is because Albus is a cat!

Dad's taken up a new hobby, yoga. Luckily, Mum seems to have given up on the bagpipes. I really miss you both I hope I can see you soon.

Loads of love,

Eva

Our cousins! ⟶

Dear Arlo and Kika,

During Lockdown I have discovered how easy it is to lose motivation in things you were once passionate about, or in things you once loved to do. Through staying at home for such an extended period I noticed everyone's routines becoming a repetitive cycle and everyone around me seemed to be programmed robots, continuously sleeping, eating and working without a single emotion or thought.

As a teenager who enjoys the freedom life gives her, I struggled to comprehend the idea of following a strict pattern and socialising only through apps and calls. I lost motivation in my studies — I had been working so hard as a GCSE student for mock exams that never seemed to be happening. By the time my mock examinations were finally announced, two weeks before I had to take them, my stress levels rose through the roof. Though I tried to stay motivated and keep working hard, I found I couldn't. I didn't keep up with my revision and the grades I worked so hard for over many months were slipping within weeks.

At this stage I felt defeated by the school system. I felt that I was drowning in a pool of work and that it was my own fault for giving up. I would go through periods of never looking up from my textbooks, to lying in bed staring at the ceiling.

When I was finally allowed to go to school my mental health improved rapidly. I realised others students were going through the same stress as me — not even just at my school but all around the world. Getting to socialise in person again gave me hope, perspective, and a reminder that Lockdown would end.

Although it hasn't been easy, I know there are people in far worse situations. For my school friends and me, the work we do over the next year will be important in shaping what comes next in our lives. I hope all students around the world will get the rewards for their hard work.

Lulu

Dear Arlo and Kika,

During Lockdown I have been walking my dogs. I have really missed playing football with my team. My sister never wants to play football with me.

I cannot wait to play with my friends.

Love Campell (age 7)

our youngest cousin!

←

Dearest grandchildren Arlo and Kika,

Our life certainly has changed dramatically during the last year.

The first Lockdown led to new pastimes. During the spring and summer last year we appreciated our garden and worked hard to make it as beautiful as it has ever been. The garden started to bloom with hydrangea pruning, summer pots and olive tree planting. We always differed on where to plant things but somehow it always got done.

We were sad not to be able to celebrate so many family birthdays, but at least by summer the rules allowed us to share our newly colourful garden with loved ones. In July we were able to go to our native Norway to see our family and friends there. That meant a great deal.

To keep occupied I (Nanny) started to bake cakes and bread for friends, neighbours and the hard-working ambulance drivers. As the NHS was struggling to provide face masks for outside wear, I started to sew them myself in cheerful colours to pass on to the brilliant staff so they could be protected on their way home. As I heard they were totally exhausted and could not sleep, I started to sew lavender bags for calming at night. That was a little contribution from me to our amazing NHS staff.

The Christmas restrictions meant that that the family could not all be together over the holidays. However, we drove down to see you before Lockdown. We came to Sussex for FIVE DAYS and ended up staying for two months! Soon after arriving, we tested positive for Coronavirus. Nanny recovered quite quickly but I (Pa) did not, ending up in hospital. I now realise how unwell I was and how worried you all were when I was taken by ambulance to Brighton Hospital. Thanks to the family and our totally wonderful NHS I recovered and am now getting fitter day by day. When I returned from hospital in mid-January there you both were to look after me and, after my isolation, you came to see me every day.

Thank you for looking after us for two months, Arlo and Kika. Your parents have been wonderful in their love, support and critical life-saving decisions and you two have been our inspiration. A silver lining for us was getting to spend such a long time with you in one go. It's been a wonderful, loving and learning experience between three generations of our family. It makes us so grateful and conscious of those less fortunate who are struggling daily with the effects of this cruel pandemic. We will miss you and all the beautiful cats, dogs, alpacas, and the early call from the duck pond.

This is a brilliant initiative, congratulations! I'm sure you will receive a lot of interesting and inspiring replies. As we come out of Lockdown, let's hope we all have learnt what is truly important in life and to be more tolerant and kinder towards other people.

Warmest love,
Nanny and Pa

Nanny and Pa are
our dad's parents

Dear Arlo and Kika,

Thank you for writing to me. Lockdown has brought many challenges to me and my family, but there have also been some positive aspects.

My friends and I were supposed to take our GCSEs in the summer of 2020, but they were cancelled. I found myself spending most of my days outside reading and baking profusely along with the majority of the country!

When school came around in September, I found life fairly normal with the exception of masks (that graced my skin with acne). The second Lockdown came and went. But the third Lockdown changed all that and we had to adapt to online classes.

Unlike most of my friends, I didn't mind studying from home. I found working more efficient and enjoyed waking up later and only minutes before my first lesson. I actually felt lucky to be at home as I was able to help my father who has been suffering with Parkinson's for nearly a decade. We spent much more time together, chatting and cooking meals, and eating lunch in our garden in the sunshine with my mother and sister. In a funny way the seclusion brought us more relaxation.

I missed playing tennis and going to the gym and cinema. I often thought about the NHS workers who have been struggling every day and how lucky my grandfather was when he fell so ill with COVID. Where would we be without our amazing NHS. I hope going forwards they are cared for and looked after, and we all come together to support each other through and after the pandemic.

Lots of love,
Harriet

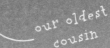 our oldest
cousin

NATURE
AND THE
ENVIRONMENT

AL GORE

Environmental activist. Author.
Former U.S. Vice President

Dear Arlo and Kika,

If we are to take only one thing away from our time spent in
Lockdown, I hope it is a better appreciation for the beauty and
fragility of the small 'blue marble' on which we live. For many
of us, the time we have been able to spend outside in nature
during this global crisis has been a powerful healing force.
But, unfortunately, this pandemic has also shown in painful
ways how our treatment of the Earth has harmed its people —
especially those who are the most vulnerable.

Many people have lived with a lot of fear during Lockdown
— fear for the health of their families and friends, fear of
whether they would be able to afford their next meal or next
month's rent, and fear of what their future might look like.
Because, as we fight off this global pandemic, we know that
the threat of our climate crisis continues to grow.

There has been a lot of time to think about — and worry about
— all of these things after more than a year of Lockdown.
But more and more, I've been reflecting less on what is so
concerning about our future, and more on what gives me hope.

YOU give me hope.

Young people like you are speaking truth to power and
demanding action for a brighter future. You are raising your
voices about the dangers of the climate crisis as if your lives
depend on it (and they do!). The power to create a more just
and greener future lies with you.

You might wonder what role you can play, when it seems like
the adults are the ones making all of the decisions. You can
use the choices you make every day to reduce your carbon
footprint. You can use your voice to encourage your family,
friends, and community to make a green future a reality. If
you're old enough, you can use your vote to protect the planet,
and if you're too young you can remind your family and friends
to vote and demand action from our leaders.

So, I ask you not to despair during these difficult times.
Just as the power of science, public service, and community
has helped get us through the pandemic, we have the ability
and the will to tackle the climate crisis. We just need to
continue doing the work.

Al Gore

MAIA ELLIOTT
Environmentalist and scientist with
ADHD/Asperger's

Dear Arlo and Kika,

Unexpectedly, the beginning of Lockdown was a magical time
for me. I had just fallen in love with an archaeologist, and when
the restrictions were announced we made the bold decision to
move in together.

We spent the spring exploring the city's hidden green spaces,
wild swimming in the river, and digging a vegetable patch in
the back garden. We noticed the lack of birds and insects, so
we sowed native wildflowers and built birdhouses. By summer,
the garden was full of life.

Those months were blissful, but things started to change when
the autumn arrived.

My job is to help make our food more sustainable, so we can reverse climate change, protect wildlife, and stop hunger. This means I often have to read and write upsetting scientific reports about the damage that our diets are doing to the natural world.

Luckily, my job also allows me to go out and meet inspiring people who are working to protect the planet, which gives me a lot of hope for the future. But because of Lockdown, I wasn't able to do this any more.

I developed intense eco-anxiety in the autumn, which made me feel incredibly lonely, despite having the love and support of my partner. I was no longer able to read or write those upsetting reports without crying, so I couldn't do my work.

One day, I saw a tiny ad for a house share in an eco-community in the countryside. Desperate to be near like-minded people again, I jumped at the opportunity, and we moved in soon after.

Today, I'm surrounded by inspiring people from all walks of life, who are united by a common desire to take care of the environment and each other. The grounds of the co-housing development are full of flowers, bird song and friendly neighbours, and the Lockdown prompted the residents to find creative new ways to have fun, make decisions together, and support one another.

If this pandemic has taught me anything, it's that life on this beautiful, fragile planet is kinder when we have community.

Love, Maia

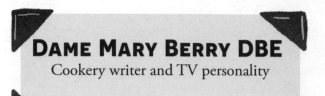

DAME MARY BERRY DBE

Cookery writer and TV personality

Dear Arlo and Kika,

What a charming letter and how wonderful to connect with everyone with 'Letters From Lockdown'.

Lockdown for me was a time to be at home, much more than I usually would, and to spend more time in the garden when the sun shone and I could appreciate nature and pottering around.

I made a point of ringing one friend a day — a friend who may be on their own or someone I may have not spoken to for a while. I felt it was important to reach out to those who may be lonely. My husband and I had each other so we were blessed. In the summer when the flowers were in bloom, I would tie a bundle with a ribbon and leave it on a neighbour's doorstep just to bring a little smile when times were tough.

My husband and I would walk the dogs every morning — our two Working Cocker Spaniels, Darcey and Freddie, who love to run through the woods. Jigsaw puzzles were a great distraction, 500 pieces is our maximum, and we have finished so many! We in fact had too many to keep so messaged our neighbours to come and collect some from the doorstep if they wished.

We clapped for carers, everyone was in our thoughts, but we were the lucky ones as we escaped COVID-19. We prayed for those who lost loved ones. 2020 will be remembered and maybe we can all learn to be a little more kind and patient.

Mary Berry

HUGH FEARNLEY-WHITTINGSTALL

Chef. Food writer. TV personality. Journalist.
Environmental campaigner

Dear Arlo and Kika,

I reckon it was only a few weeks into the first Lockdown when people began to realise that, however grim things got (and they are still very grim in many parts of the world) there were also going to be positive aspects to these extraordinary events.

We could see the benefits of less frenetic lifestyles, fewer cars on the roads, fewer planes in the sky. And we started to resolve that when we got past the immediate crisis of coping with COVID, we could do things differently, and better, in the future.

Well now is the time to unpack those resolutions and make them real. What can we do?

One thing that made a huge difference to me in the past year was witnessing the way nature seemed to leap at the opportunities we gave it. In my corner of Devon, the birdsong was louder, the wildflowers more prolific, and a walk in the countryside felt even better than it used to.

Now we can all make a resolution to give nature a bit more space.

To let a corner of our garden go wild. To not take the car when we could walk or go by bike. To pick up litter in the places we visit most often.

Of course, pretty much every decision we make impacts nature. And the way we choose to eat has some of the biggest consequences of all. If we shop locally and seasonally, eat more plants and less meat, cook more often at home instead of getting takeaways and ready meals, and waste less food, then we will be helping nature to bounce back, even as WE all bounce back. It means we are using less fossil fuel to keep us fed, and we allow nature to thrive and biodiversity to flourish on the farms that grow our food.

These may seem like small things. But there are a lot of us! And if we all do these things, the difference we make will be huge.

So let's all make small changes, and a huge difference.

With warm wishes,

Hugh Fearnley-Whittingstall

SITA BRAHMACHARI
Author

Dear Arlo and Kika,

Words, stories, songs and dreams can be superpowers. From the start I knew that 'Lockdown' wasn't a word that would help me.

'Hearth' is one of my favourite words because it contains within it so many other precious ones I love. So early on, I renamed this era we've been living through 'Virtual Hearth Time'. How many words can you find in 'Hearth'?

Loads! You'll see that there are many happy ones, some essential ones and some harsh ones too, like the times we've been living through.

I have a character in one my stories, Rima, a young girl and a refugee survivor from Syria, learning English. She tells people to 'feel about' things.

When asked if she means 'think about' things, she insists that 'feel' is the word she means.

Coming out of Virtual Hearth Time, I want to throw open so many windows and doors to take time to gather round real hearths under clear, unpolluted, starry night skies to 'feel about' the world as it has changed.

I want to remember what has been kindled with care as well as the many griefs and the need to re-feel about how we share and sustain this earth's resources.

In Virtual Hearth Time when the skies grew clear I saw how the bees came back to the disused rail track where we walked; the acts of kindness and sweetness of neighbours, friends and strangers. But mostly what I learnt about is the way we can evolve if we don't lockdown our minds and hearts.

In Virtual Hearth Time we heard loudening birdsong reaching out across this Earth. In that first spring I felt the birds' urgency — new parents protecting chicks in their nest and desperate to feed them.

I named them 'Hearth Birds'. I'll remember their call to gather round real hearths to protect all our young, long after this time has come and gone.

Sita X

Bear Grylls OBE

TV host. Author. Chief
Scout. Survivalist and outdoor
adventurer

Dear Arlo and Kika,

Thank you so much for your letter. It inspires me so much to see how young people like you are looking to the future with positivity, hope and optimism. Don't ever lose that spark. It's so key to life.

Like so many others, our family has had to adapt to this challenging year. As someone who loves the great outdoors as much as I do, I've had to get used to spending more time in the great indoors. Not always easy!

We've used the time to do things as a family that in normal times we didn't do enough of – even simple things such as going for short walks or doing an online workout together. The simple things are so important though, and little things are often really the big things – the ones that really matter. Like listening more, hugging more, cooking together more, and planning 'party nights' just us guys, watching a film or playing a silly game. All these things make for fun memories.

I've also loved doing my bit to support Scouts all across the country in my role of Chief Scout. And the most inspiring bit has been seeing how our volunteers have truly stepped up – delivering more than 1.2 million hours of fun

Scout activities on Zoom to help keep young people connected. And Scouts themselves have done some incredible things — helping raise more than a million pounds for groups and communities in need (they hiked to the moon and raced round the world all from their living rooms and gardens!).

Young people have had such a tough time this year, cut off from their friends and schools. But tough times make tough people, and I have learnt that in life it is the storms that ironically make us all stronger.

I've been so impressed by both of your courage and resilience — keep going — it counts for so much in life. Along with our brilliant NHS workers and frontline staff, you are some of the unsung heroes of Lockdown.

I am optimistic for the future as I know that it's in the hands of remarkable people like you — and more than any of us, you know that we have a duty to be smart, respectful and kind to our planet, to each other, and to make the most of every day. It's all a gift.

Well done on your inspiring project and above all, never give up.

Your friend,

Bear Grylls

CREATIVITY

CHRIS VAN DUSEN

Producer. Screenwriter. Creator of
Bridgerton, a Netflix Original Series

Over the course of these immensely challenging and unprecedented times, I would say I was, most of all, lucky. Lucky to have been in good health and spirit. Lucky to have been able to go on so many walks around the neighbourhood with my three children and husband. And, perhaps most interestingly enough, lucky to have been able to spend the majority of my Lockdown in another time and place entirely . . . That'd be 19th Century Regency London.

In March of 2020, I had just completed principal photography of the television series I created: Netflix's 'Bridgerton'. I was quickly moving into post-production while simultaneously beginning to write the show's next season. And so, for over a year (and counting), I was fortunate enough to get to momentarily leave behind the dreadful days of Lockdown by entering a new world altogether. One of glittering ballrooms and swoon-worthy country homes. One of breathtaking English gardens and some of the most beautiful, opulent palaces anyone's ever seen. There were ridiculously handsome dukes over here in this world. Young ladies who shimmered like diamonds. Eager mamas and amusing papas and commanding queens to keep them all in check.

I'll admit, it wasn't easy coming out of this imaginary world and back into the real one every night. I mean, yes, I find my husband to be just as handsome and charming as any duke. And, yes, my three little girls can (and do) keep me in check all day and all night long. Not to mention, the five of us got to promenade every single morning (okay, granted it was just down the street). But, in the lively and vibrant world known as Bridgerton, there was no pandemic. There was certainly no social distancing (try waltzing six feet apart to Vivaldi's 'Four Seasons' – let alone Ariana Grande's 'Thank You, Next'). And, of course, there was no terribly upsetting news cycle happening there. Because of all of this, my job no longer felt like a job. Instead, it became a much needed, cherished and meaningful escape. Lockdown had no place in 19th Century Regency London. But 19th Century Regency London certainly had its place in Lockdown. At least, it did for me. So, like I said: lucky.

Chris

Sir Lenny Henry CBE

Actor. Comedian. Writer

Dear Arlo and Kika,

I think it's very cool that you two are writing to a whole bunch of people. Everyone needs something to do in Lockdown.

I've been writing a lot. I love stories about magic and elves and superpowers and goblins and magicians and demons, so I'm trying to write things like that. I've written a story about a boy with wings. I bet you can't guess what it's called?

I keep busy by doing the things I've always done: I write, I think, I'm doing Grade 5 piano (it takes ages for me - I've been learning piano for years and I still can't play like Jools Holland! I want my money back).

I also read a lot. Do you like reading? I guess you do, otherwise you wouldn't be writing all these letters.

I think as long as we all look after each other, the future will be fine.

I just made a film asking my family, friends and loved ones to take the vaccine. Even though some of them are scared or worried, the film seems to have been well-received. That also began with a letter (letters are really powerful) — I wrote a letter and sent it out to a lot of people I know and they all agreed (most of them) to sign up to the message in the letter. And then a famous director made a film about it!

My brothers and sisters live in the Midlands, London, Dublin, and my friends live all over the place — but what's interesting about the Lockdown is that, even though you're not seeing everyone as regularly as you're used to, they're still on your mind. You remember that time you tried to eat an entire pineapple in one go, or that time you fell in the canal or that time you walked into a glass door. You remember how they laugh, smile, grin, play tricks on the cat, or change the rules during a game just because they're losing.

All the things you like about your friends and the people you love won't go away. They'll always be there and you'll pick up exactly where you left off. How cool will that be? Imagine it: walking into school, sitting at your desk, looking around at everyone, and the teacher says, 'Right, now where were we?'

What a lovely feeling. I bet you can't wait.

Very best wishes,

Sir Lenny Henry

HRH The Duchess of Cornwall

Dear Arlo and Kika,

Thank you very much for your extremely colourful letter. What a brilliant idea to write to one person every day during Lockdown – I'm sure you must have had some fascinating replies...!

I was particularly interested to read that you live on a farm in East Sussex – I grew up not far from you, near Plumpton, and it is one of my favourite places in the world!

You asked what I have been doing during Lockdown. Like you, I have been writing lots of letters, and I have also been working my way through a big pile of books, which I have greatly enjoyed. But I'm quite ready for Lockdown to be over now... I bet you are too!

With best wishes,

Camilla

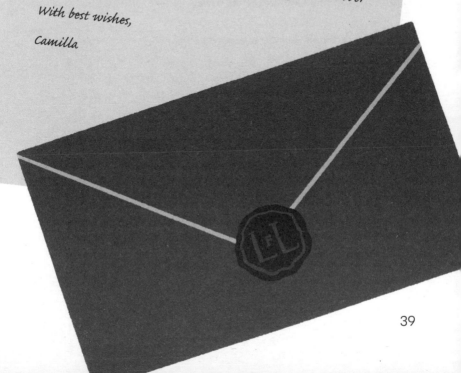

SHARNA JACKSON
Writer of words, mostly for kids.
President of the Pineapple on
Pizza Fan Club

Dear Arlo and Kika,

I hope that wherever you are, whenever you are reading this letter, you are safe, happy and looking forward to something nice to eat later.

Me? I'm good, thanks. As well as I can be. I'm writing to you from my old ship in Rotterdam. It's a special holiday here in the Netherlands today. 'Koningsdag' — the King's Birthday. People are gathering around the harbour, dipping their feet into the warmish water as it rises with the tide. As I peep though the portholes, I can see people wearing bright orange t-shirts, enjoying a drink, the sunshine and each other — at safe distances. They're reconnecting and making memories.

At the start of the pandemic, I was pretty selfish, honestly. I was working hard, and I was exhausted. At first, I was quite grateful for a moment for things to stop, for a moment to think. To talk and do less. But the more I thought, the more scared I became. I'm a fortunate person. I have somewhere safe to live, jobs that I can do from home and I'm mostly healthy. I worried about all the people who didn't have my luck and had to take many risks, so many risks.

So, I threw myself into my work, and wrote a lot. I told tall tales and escaped into the characters and worlds I created. I did think about quitting once and becoming a professional gamer because my son Joseph and I spent so much time on 'Among Us'. I thought I was good. I'm not.

I also spent a lot of time on Zoom, like I'm sure you all did. I go through cycles with Zoom, but mostly I love it — I've got to visit schools, festivals and meet people I would never have been physically and geographically able to. Sadly, Zoom funerals are also a thing now. A terrible and tragic thing. My Dad, who lives alone, and is struggling because he loves being out and active, is attending those regularly.

It's painful, but I've realised that it's OK to not always be or feel OK. The pandemic is not normal, whatever 'normal' means. It has also shown us that normal didn't always mean good, right or fair. We've learnt a lot about how people experience unfairness in our world, and I hope these are lessons we don't forget, and work together to solve.

Speaking of lessons, some of you will be back at school now. I hope you're catching up. I don't mean with your school and homework — you're not 'behind', by the way. Don't listen to anyone who says that. I mean with yourselves, your family and your friends. That's more important right now. It's the time for reconnecting and making memories. Ones that last a lifetime, and beyond.

Lots of love,

Sharna Jackson

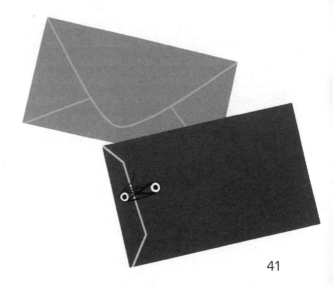

JO MALONE CBE

Founder and Creative Director, Jo Loves

Dear Arlo and Kika,

Thank you so much for your letter, which I loved reading — what a truly wonderful idea you have both come up with. It really helps to share our stories with each other, to make people laugh, cry and feel connected — WELL DONE.

I quite agree with you — the last year has been very challenging, not being able to see our friends and do the everyday things that we love. There have been a few arguments in our house too!! But they only last a few minutes, and we turn the page, forgive and carry on. I often think it is a very good way of letting off steam!

I have found the best thing during this time is to keep yourself busy, both physically — I don't know whether you have been doing PE with Joe Wicks? — but also mentally, and I am sure your home-schooling has helped in that direction.

For me, creativity has been my best friend and has kept me occupied, motivated and ready to run when this is all over. I try every day to do five things, and I wanted to share them with you:

1. Do something that makes someone really smile and feel valued.

2. Find something that makes me laugh until there are tears running down my face.

3. Walk my dog and plan for the future.

4. Create something — it might be cooking for my family, making a fragrance or writing something.

5. Dream big dreams again, pull the dreams into the day and believe they will happen.

I spend a lot of my time filling little bottles of scent and smelling them on papers and it makes me really happy.

The whole country is so very proud of your generation and how you have stood strong and fought the past year.

I wish you every success and remember: fill every day with fun and happiness, grasp every opportunity and make it yours.

Love Jo x

Sir Paul McCartney MBE

Singer. Songwriter. Musician

Dear Arlo and Kika,

Thank you for your letter – nice handwriting.

During Lockdown I have been lucky enough to be able to work in my recording studio.

I think the idea of your 'Letters From Lockdown' book is great and very thoughtful of you to help those affected by the Coronavirus.

As I say, I have been keeping busy writing songs and recording them, which I enjoy.

I believe that someday soon in the future things will start to become brighter.

Cheers,

Paul

DAME JOAN COLLINS DBE

Actress. Author. Producer. Entrepreneur.
Wife and mother

Dear Arlo and Kika,

Thank you for inviting me to contribute to this worthy cause. I dusted off my files from my early isolation and I found these few 'golden rules' I've observed about my husband's and my self-imposed seclusion:

1) **Sleep**:
   The most precious remedy to life's ills, unless your partner snores. Fortunately, we have a spare bedroom, and he can self-banish himself to help us both get our golden slumbers.

2) **Read**:
   My husband has decided that one of his projects is to clear out the basement of the great mass of books I've stored over the years, to give them to charity. The only problem with this is that I'm rediscovering many books I'd like to read again. So, while he's casually tossing them in boxes, I quietly take them away, and I have the added delight of watching his flummoxed face as the boxes do not seem to fill up.

3) **Play games**:
   I love playing games (as evidenced above, but also more traditional games) such as poker, gin rummy and Scrabble. The only issue with this is that if one partner is more adept (me) it can lead to bickering.

4) **Watch TV**:
   There are a myriad of great, and also a myriad of ghastly, offerings now on TV and every possible viewing platform (Netflix, Amazon, BritBox

etc.) BritBox actually offers some fabulous British vintage fare to watch: 'Upstairs, Downstairs' – much better than today's period pieces; 'Fawlty Towers' – utterly brilliant yet politically incorrect, but so what? Any films with Barbara Stanwyck or Robert de Niro. I even found a boxset of 'Dynasty', which was really quite amusing actually, and has great clothes!

5) **A further word on watching TV:**
This, of course, requires something called the internet. My husband, the prophet of doom, remarked that he doubted this internet thingy would be able to hold out much longer with everyone putting a strain on it. Two days ago, he burst into the room exclaiming, 'See? I was right. The internet is dead!' 'What can I do? Can I help?' I replied – more to be supportive than to actually help, you understand. He grunted and left the room. A few minutes later, on the way to the kitchen I noticed something unusual. 'Darling,' I said, in my most placatory tone, 'Isn't that white thingy supposed to be plugged in?'

6) **Economize:**
Tin foil is washed if dirty and neatly folded for re-use, loo rolls and soap sparingly used, boxes saved. Such economies keep us busy for hours.

7) **Exercise:**
Another great cure for all ills, exercise is key but can also be a source of resentment. My husband has been on a health kick for almost a year, and he will wake up early for a run and come home flushed with

virtuous accomplishment, whilst I lay in bed reading ALL the papers, sipping my second cup of coffee. Whilst his smug face seems to say, 'So, when are YOU getting moving?' I contemplate throwing the contents of my cup at him. But then I think better of it – waste of coffee.

8) Chat to all my friends and family:

Nothing is more important (particularly when 'A Hubby' seesaws between doom-mongering and virtuousness) than being in touch with other people. Particularly when they convey humorous observations of this new world. 'It's amazing,' a friend remarked to me, 'judging from the supermarket shelves in Hollywood, how few gluten allergies there seem to be now.'

9) Cook:

My husband and I are finding novel ways of using beans, pulses and items that, frankly, I never knew we had in the cupboards. But beware not finishing everything on the plate. 'That's at least 100 grams of pasta you've left on your plate,' he scolds at me, 'and the supermarket shelves are empty.' I gently point out that if he hadn't served me enough to feed a rugby squad, there might not be so much left over.

10) Write:

There is nothing I enjoy more than observing our foibles and fancies and putting them down on paper, as I have done here!

Love, Joan XXX

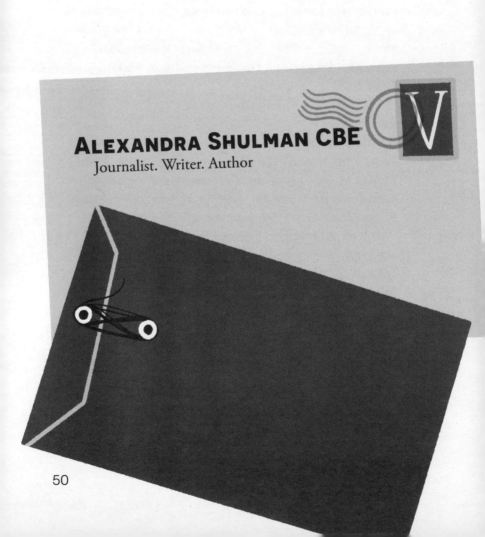

ALEXANDRA SHULMAN CBE

Journalist. Writer. Author

Dear Arlo and Kika,

Thank you for inviting me to contribute to 'Letters From Lockdown' — great idea.

I have been lucky, as no one in my close family has been very ill and we all have homes to spend time in. <u>BUT</u> I don't think humans are made to live in tiny groups and I miss my friends and going out and having fun — a lot.

Like everyone, I have good and bad days, so I have tried to come up with some plans to make it a bit easier. Here are a few things I have discovered:

1. It is vital to get dressed. No pyjamas by midday or it becomes too depressing.

2. Making soup (which I never did before) is a soothing activity.

3. I allow myself to watch as much TV as I want.

4. I have read books about things I would not normally — a history of pineapples, an anthology of the weather. Information that is unusual is good to know!

5. A vodka gimlet — ½ vodka, ½ lime cordial, lots of ice — at 7.30pm is delicious. You'll have to try one when you're older!

6. I make a timetable each day for all my tasks — and stick to it. It helps.

Good luck,
Alexandra

Ed Sheeran MBE
Musician

Dear Arlo and Kika,

Thanks very much for your letter, and what a fantastic idea!

Lockdown for me was a year of changes. Most notably, I became a father to a wonderful little firework of joy called Lyra. You would love her — she's very smiley and loves to dance.

We found out about her just before Lockdown began, so in the first few months I was prepping stuff for her arrival. I ordered a bunch of cherry wood from a guitar company who makes my guitars in Northern Ireland, and with this cherry wood I made Lyra a cot! It took me around a month, and because I hadn't done woodwork since I was at school (when I was probably not much older than you), it was a slow trial and error process. But the finished result is great, and it's lovely to see it being used by Lyra every night and during nap time.

I spent the rest of the time working on music, trying to write a song or two a day just about anything I was feeling that day. I think the album is good and I can't wait for you to hear it. Also, I got into painting! I don't know if you saw my cover for my last song, 'Afterglow', but I painted that in Lockdown. It's so fun just chucking paint at a canvas and seeing what happens while getting covered in it during the process.

Like the rest of the world, me and my family have had many ups and downs this last year. I hope yours has had more ups than downs, and I think your book idea is a wonderful one.

Lots of love,

Ed xx

RESILIENCE

DR ANUSHUA GUPTA
Mum. Wife. GP. COVID fighter.
Rehab enthusiast. Netflix addict.
#NeverGiveUp

Dear Arlo and Kika,

My name is Anushua Gupta. I am a medical doctor
in Manchester, UK. I am married to Ankur, also
a doctor and we have a daughter called Ariana,
who was only 18 months old when I was admitted to
hospital with COVID-19 in March 2020; two weeks
after my 40th birthday. On 4th April 2020, I became
critically unwell. I was intubated, ventilated and
was in a medically induced coma for around two
months.

Ten days later, I deteriorated further. I had to
be started on ECMO (extracorporeal membrane
oxygenation) to give me any chance of survival. It
is a machine that does the work of the lungs while
the lungs repair themselves from the damage caused
by severe COVID-19 infection. I was one of the first
patients to go on ECMO for COVID-19 in the UK. I was
on ECMO for 34 days. Around late May 2020 I started
to show signs of improvement. I have been told that
it was nothing short of a miracle that I survived.

As I woke from the coma, I realised I had no voice, I wasn't able to swallow, and I could barely move my limbs or do anything for myself. Due to the Lockdown regulations, my husband and daughter were unable to come and visit me in hospital. It was so difficult for all three of us that we could not be together for such a long time. I longed to hold and hug my baby. This made me feel so low and anxious.

I had to have intense physiotherapy, speech and language therapy, and psychotherapy as part of my rehabilitation. I came home after 150 days in hospital. I restarted working two and a half months after coming home. My daughter and my family have been my driving force. I am now raising money to buy specialist equipment for the rehabilitation teams at the hospital where I was a patient.

I am unsure of how and where I contracted COVID-19 but I know my role working as a frontline worker certainly placed me in a higher risk category. As medical professionals, passionate about looking after sick patients, we sacrifice our own lives and put at risk the lives of our families when we go to work. Being on the opposite side as a patient consolidated how hard medical professionals are working to save lives during these unprecedented times. I am so grateful to the hospital staff who cared for me. I am here and alive due to their outstanding level of care.

Yours sincerely,
                    Anushua

ADRIAN PACKER CBE

CEO of CORE Education Trust, Birmingham

Dear Arlo and Kika,

I was very happy to hear from you and to be asked to contribute to your brilliant 'Letters From Lockdown' idea. As someone who is responsible for running schools, I think it is extremely important for children and young people to find creative new ways to stay busy and inspired, now more than ever.

I was particularly interested to hear that as brother and sister you have been trying not to argue. It's natural to feel these emotions because so many of the things we enjoy have been taken away: playing sports and games; going to events with our friends; travelling to new places and even seeing other family members. This can seem quite unfair.

You asked about what I've been doing this past year. I've had the great privilege of leading and supporting the teachers I work with here in Birmingham. They have been using this time to think of others, for example by delivering food parcels to families and going the extra mile to make sure our students are safe and well. Unfortunately, many of our students and their families have had to cope with food poverty and going without the basics so sadly there is only so much we can do in the current challenging circumstances. You may have heard about a very sad incident in Birmingham where a child

Arlo and Kika

died after being attacked near to where he lived. Some of the staff in one of my schools used to teach this boy. This tragic news was particularly difficult for us to hear because we all felt so helpless. Teachers are naturally protective. We have found being apart from our students incredibly hard.

Despite the difficulties and tragedies we've faced recently, I feel all teachers have a duty to look forward with optimism and to focus on a happier, brighter future. As more children like you return to school, we will all need to adjust again. We need to remember that we've all had to face challenges, and that these will have been different for every community, every family, and for every individual adult, young person and child. I think this period of adjustment will bring the best out of us all. We will be kinder, more caring and more thoughtful of other people.

Too many people talk about your generation being 'left behind' by the pandemic. I disagree. I think your generation will lead the way in looking forward with new optimism, ambition and unity. Our job as teachers will be to support you create that future and to make sure our schools become places of possibility once again .

With peaceful best wishes to you and all your family,

Adrian

PAUL ATHERTON

(FRSA) has been homeless for the past 12 years
but has remained a successful film-maker,
playwright, journalist and artist

Dear Arlo and Kika,

Thank you so much for writing to me.

Being homeless in Lockdown was both good and bad.

To begin with, it was very bad. I use the hard seats in Heathrow Airport Terminal 5 as my bed each night. I'm sure you can imagine how uncomfortable and difficult it is to sleep sitting upright, and how hard it is to sleep for long with all the lights on and the noise of all the people passing by all night.

So, when the Prime Minister said everybody had to stay inside, instead of coming into Trafalgar Square in Central London every day, as I usually did, I had to stay in the airport all the time.

I suspect when you get up you just walk into the bathroom and have a wash and clean your teeth. Well, there are no showers available to me at the airport, so I have to travel an hour by tube to Kings Cross, walk 5 minutes to a local gym there and pay £2.50 just to get a shower. Being locked in at the airport meant I couldn't do that.

But after a few weeks the good news came and we were all offered hotel rooms to stay in. I was given a hotel apartment, which meant I could sleep lying down, shower every day, cook and eat healthy food and exercise. I felt much, much better than I had done for a very long time. I've not had a home for 12 years.

Many people think being homeless means you've done something bad or stupid and it's your own fault you are sleeping rough. It isn't. We live in a very silly society at the moment. The laws that are meant to protect us from harm, sometimes are written just to protect people from losing money. It's why it is so crazily expensive to buy or rent a place to live at the moment.

And it is also the reason why I will be back sleeping at Heathrow again very soon. Because I'm ill I can't work, and the government doesn't want to spend money helping people like me.

If you ever see anyone on the street asking people for money, always smile at them and say hello if you are with your parents...they will most likely have done nothing wrong to find themselves there and a little kindness goes a very, very long way when you don't have a home. It won't cost you a penny.

All best wishes,

Paul

COLETTE MOREIRA-HENOCQ
Residential care manager. Family orientated.
Workaholic. Dog-lover

Dear Arlo and Kika,

It's been a complicated time of late, the world was closed: shops, pubs, clubs. My world however, the world of healthcare, was very much open all hours. For me the days carried on, I got up and went to work, then went back home. After a while work started to become stressful. It was hard watching and caring for people who were poorly, knowing that nobody else could come in and see them. You had to be strong all the time, not only for the residents you cared for but also for their families and for your colleagues.

I started to feel alone and the pressure of work was getting to me. That's when I realised one other thing had closed — my parents' front door. I couldn't visit, which meant I couldn't vent or have somewhere else to go when my day was just a little too much. I began to feel homesick despite not having lived there for seven years; I just wanted to go 'home'.

I started to call my mum and dad often, and as a result I learnt that both my sisters were feeling a similar way to me. Eventually we forged what we call 'family facetime' which would happen either on Friday or Saturday evenings. Each

household would take turns organising the games for that evening, and we used to play with the array of filters.
My sisters and I were convinced that our mum would have had enough of us chatting halfway through, as we always ended up facetiming the ceiling! Despite being held apart by Lockdown, I can't help feeling that we became closer as a family.

I guess Lockdown was not all bad, although times were hard, good things came of it: home improvements and spending time with my three dogs Tuga, Tallulah and Toffee. It gave me a chance to reflect on the importance of health and of family. Perhaps after the Lockdown we will never be back to 'normal' but maybe that's not such a bad thing. Maybe this gives us an opportunity to create a new normal, a more caring, considerate, environmentally appreciative normal.

Fingers crossed.

Colette

NEERA BUTT

Cleaning supervisor, Rockwood Academy,
Birmingham

Dear Arlo and Kika,

Thank you so much for sending me your letter. I feel very privileged to be part of this.

My name is Neera Butt and I am the cleaning supervisor at Rockwood Academy in Birmingham. The cleaning team and I have worked tirelessly throughout COVID-19, ensuring the school is as safe and clean as possible for all teaching staff and students. I am so proud of my team and the school for working as hard as they have throughout these difficult times.

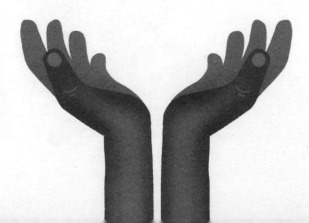

When COVID-19 broke out in March 2020, like everyone else I was alarmed and scared. I wanted to know how I could protect my family and how I could protect myself. I needed to have the right information and support. I looked to the government, my employer, and my friends and family for help. When I went to work I had so many questions: Do I have to come to work or do I not? How will this affect me and my family financially? If I come to work, will I be safe?

As a key worker, I felt that I had all the support that I needed to protect myself and my family. My focus was my faith as a Muslim woman: I made the decision that I would work hard and help others and leave my fate in the hands of my religion. This, with the help of my family, took away the fear of the unknown.

I am lucky to have taken part in testing on a regular basis, and to this day I have not been infected by COVID-19, and for that I am eternally grateful. But during this time, my husband has been severely ill with a separate health issue. With the restrictions and limitations that are in place, it has proven challenging to support him and my immediate family. However, it has brought us together and we've given each other strength.

I am extremely hopeful that as our national Lockdown begins to lift our lives will begin to return to normal. Whether this will be the normal that we knew, or a new normal, I am optimistic for what it will bring.

I am sincerely sorry to those individuals who have lost loved ones – my deepest sympathy extends to them all.

Thank you again for giving me this opportunity to contribute my voice.

Yours sincerely,

Neera Butt

KAREN POLLOCK CBE
Chief Executive, Holocaust Educational Trust

Dear Arlo and Kika,

Thank you for your letter. Lockdown has been difficult for many people and I am grateful that my family and I remain safe and well despite the challenges.

I love going out and meeting new people, so I've had to adapt quite a bit. I didn't make any banana bread, but I certainly got into cooking and I love cycling at home to loud music!

I run the Holocaust Educational Trust and we work to ensure that young people know about the Holocaust. During the Second World War, when Hitler's Nazi Party and allies set out to destroy the Jewish people of Europe, some managed to escape to safety, but many families were not able to leave. Jewish lives and communities were completely destroyed. Other minority groups were also targeted for persecution. It is our job to make sure that these horrors are never forgotten and that we understand where hate and prejudice can lead.

One of the hardest things about studying this period in history is confronting how humans could inflict such cruelty. We work with teachers, ensuring that they are confident to teach about this difficult history in schools, and we are especially privileged to work with Holocaust survivors — people who lived through these awful times.

Our survivors are amazing. Of course, this year has brought challenges for them as it has for many of us. They have not been able to see their family and have not been able to be as independent as they would like, and they have missed their friends. But they are strong and resilient. Many tell us they have experienced something far worse in their lifetimes and on the whole they have managed Lockdown with their typical optimism and determination.

What is particularly tough for the survivors is not being able to visit schools. In normal times, they speak to thousands of people every week in classrooms up and down the country, sharing their difficult memories. They inspire the young people who hear their stories and in turn they are inspired by the students they meet. They do this so that their loved ones who died are remembered. Thankfully, many have adapted to using technology, so they can continue to share their testimony. Even with the challenges of Lockdown, I am certain their stories will be carried into the future, and what happened to the Jewish people over 75 years ago will never be forgotten.

Despite everything they have been through, the survivors are the most life-affirming people I know. Any cause for celebration they grab, and rightly so. Lockdown has reminded us that these precious eyewitnesses will not be here forever; that we need to value their testimonies and plan for the future. We need to make sure that everyone knows what happened during the Holocaust so we can prevent antisemitism, racism and hate.

It is the determination and spirit of the survivors of the Holocaust that has kept me going during this year and I cannot wait to see them again. It is up to us all to make sure that their legacies live on.

Karen Pollock

DAWN BILBROUGH

NHS critical care nurse

Dear Arlo and Kika,

My name is Dawn and I live in North Yorkshire. My favourite thing is to spend time outdoors with my very happy dog Wilma, a chocolate-coloured spaniel, who is always ready for an adventure.

Like you, I also enjoy spending precious time with my friends and have missed them during the pandemic. They're usually such a big part of my life and not being able to hug them has felt incredibly strange and at times lonely.

My work is within Intensive Care, a special department in hospital that takes care of the sickest patients. As a nurse I work within a team that aims to get people well enough to return home to their families and friends.

In 2020 when patients with COVID began to arrive, like many I was afraid of this unknown virus. Scientists were working hard but there was little information available. There was concern for the safety of my patients and my family. In the beginning I was unsure if the virus would follow me home.

The intensive care unit quickly became full and other departments within the hospital were used to ensure care could be provided to everyone who needed specialist treatment.

Working through the pandemic has been a sad time. Despite doctors and nurses working tirelessly, too many people died, never to return home to their families or friends.

Being witness to this produced a wave of emotions. I would often wake with an emptiness in the pit of my stomach. Family and friends have continued to show their love and listened patiently as I expressed my feelings through my story, helping to heal my sadness.

Each day feels a little lighter now, the emptiness in my stomach has disappeared, replaced with immense gratitude. I will always be thankful that many people worked incredibly hard to create a vaccine that will keep people safe from COVID-19.

At hospital we now receive news from those patients who survived the virus and have finally made it home to their loved ones. I am sure you will agree, this is truly happy news.

Love and best wishes,

Dawn Bilbrough (Wilma's Bestie).

PC HOLLIE LONG
Police Constable, Force Intelligence and
Specialist Operations Unit, Thames Valley
Police

Dear Arlo and Kika,

Being a frontline police officer, nothing really shocks me any more — I have
seen the good, the bad, and everything in-between. Then COVID-19 happened
and changed what I thought I knew.

I've always been an emergency worker but now I was a 'key worker'.
However, for the police this meant a responsibility to enforce new laws,
restrict freedoms, and put ourselves at even more risk.

Used to working as a team, I was suddenly alone and have been for a year.
I get up, get into my police vehicle, do my job, then I go home, often not
seeing another officer all day. I don't have a morning briefing, or a coffee
and a catch up with my team any more — it is those little things, the
motivation boosters, that I miss. My life has become my job.

The majority of people have showed willingness to help us as we try to keep
people safe, understanding the bigger picture. Some communities have really
rallied together which has been lovely to see. Sadly, other people spit and

cough in officers' faces and laugh that they are spreading the virus. At a time when we should all be standing together, I saw a clear division between decent people and the self-centred ones. I have been busy dealing with criminals who are seemingly oblivious a global pandemic is in full swing, and those people scare me far more than the 'gangsters' who threaten me with knives!

The rules were confusing for us too. I have been out there keeping families safe whilst not being able to hug mine. It's been a frustrating and mentally tough time for all, but fortunately for me, I did not join the police force for recognition; I joined to keep people safe from the monsters out there. I'll never know if I have fully succeeded at that, but I'd like to think I've made a difference. I hope that, despite adverse media coverage and constant scrutiny, the public knows that my colleagues and I in blue are the good guys.

Hollie Long

Dr Jenny Messenger

Consultant Respiratory Physician,
Brighton

Dear Arlo and Kika,

Thank you so much for your lovely letter. It has given me the opportunity to reflect on everything that has happened.

It seems like only yesterday that I first heard about the coronavirus outbreak in China. As a respiratory doctor I had, of course, already heard about SARS and MERS. This would be the same, right? Just something we would need to know about on the off chance we might get a case in our hospital.

Then suddenly the cases started to appear in the UK. People were getting very sick. My colleagues and friends started to worry and a genuine state of panic started to set in.

In Brighton we were about two weeks behind things in London. We heard that colleagues were getting sick and some were even dying. People like us. People like me. It felt like time stood still as we all waited and then suddenly it arrived.

I had to isolate initially as my twin boys had a fever. It was so hard not being at work and I was so worried about my colleagues having to face it and felt so helpless. I heard of colleagues too worried to go home in case they might give it to their families. One had been sleeping in a shed in his garden. Would my family be okay?

At home I was frantically writing policies and protocols for this new disease we had no real idea how to manage. Overnight our clinics were cancelled. As a lung cancer physician, what would happen to all my patients and how could I look after them now? What was the plan?

The next few weeks were a blur of ward rounds in full protective equipment. It was like living your life behind a screen. I started to see my cancer patients again and had to learn to break bad news with a mask and visor on. No longer being able to touch or even be close to them at this terrible time. They didn't even have a loved one with them.

I am sorry to say that in this country it is not uncommon to see our patients die alone, without any family or friends to hold their hands. During this pandemic this was so much worse.

You asked whether I feel positive about the future. The answer of course is yes. I've seen how this difficult time has brought out the very best in people. How communities have pulled together. The generosity and selflessness we can all be capable of. People in the NHS, carers and other key workers were voluntarily risking their lives for strangers. After all, helping to make people better and return them to their loved ones is why everyone in healthcare does what they do.

I hope the end is in sight for us and I hope we will soon be back to being able to spend time with our friends and family.
The world will be a better place as I am sure we will all have learnt so much from this experience and I hope that we can hang on to those things to make a better future
for you, our next generation.

Love,

Jenny

FRIENDS
AND
FAMILY

DAME JACQUELINE WILSON DBE

Children's writer. Total bookworm.
Owned by a cat and dog

Dear Arlo and Kika,

It's been such a strange time, hasn't it? At first Lockdown seemed very scary, even for adults, and we got really worried. But gradually we've all got used to staying at home and wearing our masks when we go out and keeping at a proper distance when we see our friends. Now I'd say we mostly find Lockdown simply boring, because every day seems to be the same.

I've missed seeing my daughter most of all. She's grown up now and lives a long way away from me. I know she's fine and she gets in touch frequently – but I just want to see her and hug her and spend time with her! I wonder who you've missed the most?

I've missed my friends and all our chats and fun and laughter. I've missed going to have a long browse in a bookshop or swimming in a big pool or having a wander round an art gallery. However, I haven't missed going out to work, because I'm a

writer and I always work from home. I've got a lovely study (though I mostly write my books in the morning sitting up in bed in my pyjamas!).

I'm also lucky enough to have a special partner, a lively dog and a cuddly cat, so I've still had plenty of company. We live in the country and so we've had really long interesting walks – but I used to live in a town and know it's difficult when you just have the same park to trudge round each day.

For some families, life has changed forever. Jobs have been lost, and beloved relatives have sadly passed away. But wherever you live, whatever your circumstances, life will get back to normal one day (soon I hope!). Keep safe and keep your spirits up too.

Love from Jacqueline

THE MARSH FAMILY

A family of six from Kent who used musical
parody to sing about life during Lockdown

Dear Arlo and Kika,

The last year has been a strange one for our family, because
although we have been cut off from people for long periods, we
have also managed to make friends all over the world!

Music has always been a family hobby. From the time the
children were small, we have created songs and videos for
family and friends. As the kids have grown, so have their
musical talents, so when we went into Lockdown last March, we
decided to create a video of us doing a parody of a song from
the musical 'Les Mis' that Ben (my husband) had changed
the lyrics to. We recorded ourselves on a Sunday afternoon
— argument and all! — then posted our 'One Day More' video
on Ben's Facebook and tagged family and friends who were
having birthdays we would miss.

We woke the next morning to find the video had 'gone viral'
and millions of people had viewed it! We rode a rollercoaster of
interviews and requests over the next two weeks and got the
most amazing messages from people who had suffered losses or
been working long shifts in hospitals or were struggling with

being alone. It made us feel like we were making a difference and we encouraged people to donate money to the WHO COVID-19 fund along with our own appearance fees.

We set up our own YouTube channel and continued to put out songs which were based on our own frustrations or lockdown experiences. Then in January we recorded 'Have the New Jab', encouraging people to have the vaccine, and we started a fundraiser for Save the Children. In February we recorded our take on Bonnie Tyler's 80s classic which we called 'Totally Fixed Where We Are'. Crazily, it went viral again and we were contacted by the people at Comic Relief and asked to perform on their live show. We were thrilled that our own fundraising, which we boosted with ad revenue from another song we wrote called 'We're Not Singing Sea Shanties', made over £13,000 for Red Nose Day.

Our videos have all had one mistake (or several) in them, but we try and show the reality of family life and the challenges of getting six people to perform at the same time. Our videos have been a great distraction for us and they also seem to have helped other people express frustrations, recognise their own concerns or just laugh a little. The pandemic has been difficult for everyone but we have felt some amazing unity with people around the world and a shared desire for a better future. This is something we've really cherished!

Much Love,

The Marsh Family xx

BORIS JOHNSON MP

Prime Minister of the
United Kingdom

Dear Arlo and Kika,

Thank you so much for inviting me to take part in your fantastic 'Letters From Lockdown' project.

It's brilliant that you have been writing to a different person every day, collecting stories from around the world and raising money for a great cause.

I also write a letter every day to thank those in our country who are doing something special to help others, by recognising them as a Point of Light.

So today I am delighted to recognise you both as the UK's 1,680th and 1,681st Points of Light. Congratulations!

I have been very busy leading the country's response to Coronavirus and, like your dad, I was ill with it for a while. But our fantastic National Health Service helped me to get better.

When I am not working, Carrie and I love spending time with our baby boy, Wilfred, and our dog, Dilyn. We have a garden at the back of Downing Street where we all play together and when I have the time I also go out for a run or a bike ride. I find that exercise helps me feel well and one of the things I have learnt after being ill is that we all need to try and keep ourselves fit!

In answer to your question about whether I have a positive outlook on the future, I say: yes, absolutely! I believe we can build back better from this horrible virus, not just recovering but actually finding ways to make life better than it was before.

I also think that in some ways Lockdown has brought out the best in people – and I am sure your book will be filled with wonderful stories of amazing things that people have done. I can't wait to read it!

Congratulations again on becoming Points of Light and good luck with the book launch in July!

Boris Johnson

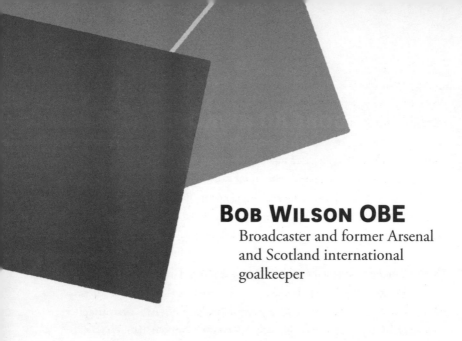

Bob Wilson OBE

Broadcaster and former Arsenal
and Scotland international
goalkeeper

Dear Arlo and Kika,

What a great project you have come up with. And an equally wonderful
charity in Barnardo's to support and raise money for.

Lockdown has been a challenge for everyone and that definitely includes me:
someone who was lucky enough to be born with huge energy, and a need to fill
each day and make the most of it. That said, gone are the days when I would
throw myself around a goalmouth at Arsenal. Action man! That was me.

Lockdown has made me realise and appreciate what a 'lucky boy' I've been
throughout my life, especially with family and friends, the two most important
aspects of life as far as I'm concerned.

My Scottish mum and dad lived through two world wars and taught me about
respect, good manners and much more, including how to face loss and sadness.
The two eldest of their six children were both killed serving in the RAF in
World War II. Jack, my eldest brother was just 19 when his Spitfire was shot
down. I was 4 months old. Billy, a rear gunner in a Lancaster bomber, was just

20 when he failed to return home. These were my two 'hero' brothers who I have no recollection of outside the family photos, incredible last letters home, and the various sporting trophies and medals they gained in growing up.

As for my other brothers, Don and Hugh, and my sister Jean, I have leant on them by being the youngest. Leant on, learnt from and loved. I've had time in Lockdown to dive into my family files, laughing about my childhood days, my university years, my 'Roy of the Rovers' years at Arsenal and then my 28 years surviving at the BBC and ITV as a self-trained sports presenter.

Our files and books also brought some sadness and a tear or two. Tears of happiness and joy with my remarkable wife, Megs, reflecting on our children becoming adults. All three became successful in their chosen occupations. John, a BBC Radio presenter; Rob, a commercial photographer; and Anna, a Community Nursing Sister. We reflected on their early days, the crazy fun-filled holidays we all spent together, as well as their respective marriages, and our grandchildren. As for tears, well, that surrounds Anna's fight for life against a rare form of cancer. Tears, and also pride at how she fought. Always smiling, always thinking and caring about us first, her family. Of course, we miss Anna. Every day, irrevocably, our lives have changed. Except she is still with us, her smile, her love of life, her letters. All wrapped up and contained in my new 'Lockdown' files.

I'm grateful to be reminded of everyone and everything that makes life so memorable, wonderful and worthwhile.

Good luck with your book.

Lots of Love,

Bob xx

PEPPA PIG

A fan of muddy puddles.
Oink oink!

Dear Arlo and Kika

Thank you for writing to me.

It must be sooooo nice to live on a farm! I bet you have
lots of animals and ducks and frogs and all sorts. We
don't have any animals, just Goldie who is a goldfish.
Granny and Grandpa have Polly Parrot who we haven't
been able to see because Granny and Grandpa are in
Lockdown too!

Mummy and Daddy are BOTH working from home
which is brilliant because it means we can play
every day. Daddy has been doing lots and
lots of cooking, which Mummy says has
made the kitchen very clean because
he's very good at tidying up! Mummy
has been doing lots of
work on the computer
which is sooooo
boring.

We haven't been able to see any of our friends, but I speak to my best friend Suzie Sheep every day on the phone.

George and I play outside lots of the time and because it has been raining, we have been able to do my most favourite thing:

Jumping up and down in Muddy Puddles!

But remember . . .

If you jump in muddy puddles you must wear your boots.

George says 'Grrr' and hopes your book raises lots of money for children who are not as lucky as us. Mummy is helping me write this letter as I'm a bit too little to spell the words right.

Lots of love,

Peppa Pig
Oink Oink!

ED BALLS

Broadcaster. Writer. Economist.
Professor. Former Shadow
Chancellor of the Exchequer

Dear Arlo and Kika,

Thank you for your lovely letter. It really cheered me up. I was having a boring Lockdown day when it arrived – like you I really miss seeing my friends and going out on trips.

I bet you've missed going to school. My youngest daughter is doing her A Levels and I've been impressed by how her school has organised teaching online. But I will feel much better about the future when I know that all children are going to get extra learning time, so no-one falls behind.

Our two oldest kids had to come home when the pandemic started and I cooked dinner every evening for the whole family. After a while I got a bit bored and started trying new recipes, but they told me off: 'Stop doing all this new stuff, just cook the things we like'.

I've missed seeing my mum who lives in a care home a long way away from me. I haven't been able to visit for over a year. She has dementia and needs people close by to touch and see. So video calls don't work so well for her.

But otherwise Zoom and Teams have been brilliant. Last week I spoke at a book launch at St Andrew's University in Scotland via my computer while, at the same time, I was also at my daughter's parents' forum on my phone. No-one knew except me!

And my brother, sister and I have been able to do a Zoom call every day with my dad during Lockdown – once he had worked out to use his phone! I've spoken to him more in the last year than the previous twenty years combined. It's funny how being apart has, in some ways, made us closer.

I missed our kids very much when the Lockdown eased and they went off to university. But that's what it's like being a parent as your kids get older. With the vaccine working so well, young people a little older than you will soon be back playing and learning and travelling far and wide, knowing there is always home to come back to. Which is how things should be.

Best wishes,

Ed

HAYDEN KAYS
British artist. Born 1985

Dear Arlo and Kika,

Hello tomorrow, remember yesterday? Nah, not really, it's all so similar nowadays. Feels like another Blursday afternoon.

I sleep a lot, clean a lot, cook a lot, eat a lot. Typing and tapping into my phone. I'm still working hard, just from home now.

I've got used to adapting and clapping, weeping at the news; polarising opinions and some troubling views. Cancel culture, anti-bac, anti-vax, all socially distanced. We've talked of immunity, furlough, BLM and social resistance. 'Flatten the curve' and the need for 'personal protective equipment'. I just miss hanging out with my brother and sisters. My mother and father and grandmas, we've never experienced such distance. Zoom in, zoom out. It's a weak connection at the best of times. 'I miss you. There's nothing like having you here.'

Social media keeps me entertained and emotionally drained.
Kittens and memes, lots of men falling over. But also spite-
filled reactions and misunderstandings. Banana bread laced
with existential dread. I've reached my limit, that is for sure.
Must put down the phone and get out the door.

The new normal. Nothing genuinely new is ever normal.
Normality is familiarity. The lack of familiarity has enabled
some clarity. Less flights, no traffic, silenced honking horns.
We hear nature is healing, but this seems far too premature.
'It's mad isn't it?' is all we seem to hear. The occasional jogger
wobbles past the window. Now is the time for total character
reinvention. Get fit, stop that, start this. 'Just one sec, I'm
about to complete Netflix.' No news is good news, but this time
it's bad. Tsunami of statistics – this many, that many, how
many, too many.

Right. That's enough. It's taking its toll. I must throw myself
into painting and drawing, it's medicinal for my sanity. An
instant boundless travel card to an alternate reality. More
time with my fiancée, Louise, the day to start a family we
seize. It grew a little with Sneaky The Cat, but we were never
going to be content with just that. We've made a contribution
to the 'Lockdown Generation'. A brand-new consciousness,
blissfully oblivious to all of this.

Hayden

WOODY

A cowboy sheriff with a pull-string, working tirelessly to make sure his kid and friends are safe and well. Woody recently embarked on a new journey, saying 'so long, partner' to best-bud Buzz Lightyear for a new life with his friend Bo Peep

Hey Howdy Hey!

Just wanted to send you a note on how Bo and I are doing these days. When the world went topsy-turvy last year, we decided to hunker down with some of the other carnival toys and most importantly, stay together as a team! It hasn't always been easy, but one thing is for sure: we've all gotten to know each other pretty darn well. Everyone is doing their best to stay positive and try to have a little fun together ... And it's made me realise that sometimes you don't truly appreciate the things (or the toys) around you, 'til life throws you for a loop.

Anyhow, maybe we'll start travelling again soon, or maybe even find our way back to Bonnie's room ... I really miss Buzz and the gang. Whatever happens next, we've still got each other!

Your pal,

Woody

THE
UNEXPECTED

MEGGIE FOSTER
Actress

Dear Arlo and Kika,

Isn't Lockdown just the worst? If you're anything like me, sitting
still – never mind being told to stay indoors for almost a year – is
a total nightmare. When Boris Johnson first announced we would
be confined to Zoom, socially distanced 'EastEnders' and the
muscular flexing of Joe Wicks I imagined 2020 would be the most
boring year (well, apart from Joe). But actually *whispers it* it
turned out to be one that would completely change my life.

It all started when I sat down to watch the news. 'Why would
you do that?', you might ask. Obviously, it was a complete misery
fest, not least because of these strange martian creatures talking
gibberish on our screens. You know . . . politicians.

Politicians like to think they shape our destinies. And don't tell
anyone, but they shaped mine. That is, when I decided I would give
their job a go . . . My sessions began as some fun – I donned a wig,
grabbed my microphone, gave my best Boris Johnson caricature,
and then posted it on Twitter. That's when things really exploded!
Appropriately, the virus made me viral.

Perhaps this wasn't a complete coincidence. Growing up I always knew I wanted to be an actress, although I certainly didn't go in thinking it would be easy. Before 2020 I was close to giving up. But sometimes you don't know what's around the corner. Even if it's inspiration from a seemingly drunk politician stumbling over her numbers at the COVID-19 daily briefing.

Since then, I've had a blast making more videos and have been lucky enough to be featured in various newspapers, magazines, and even ended up on 'Lorraine'. Although I confess it's not always sunshine, lollipops and rainbows. It turns out it's not just politicians who 'haters gonna hate', as Taylor Swift would say — but I've tried to rise above it!

What I learnt the most is that life can be surprising. Even when you're bored, sad or just want to go to a restaurant again, never lose sight of the bigger picture. Lockdowns, though annoying, aren't permanent. Dreams last forever, though.

Stay safe.

All my love,

Meggie Foster
xxxxx

DAVEY GLOVER
Train Manager, LNER.
Terrifically tall. Cat Dad.
Chocoholic

Dear Arlo and Kika,

My name is Davey and I am a Train Manager for LNER. I carry out the train guard duties, which include the safe dispatch of the train from stations and looking after the customers onboard, while checking tickets and railcards. I work on the East Coast Mainline and my regular routes are between London King's Cross and Leeds, Newcastle, Lincoln and Kingston-upon-Hull. I normally have 500 – 600 passengers on my train but during Lockdown the trains were very quiet.

In one way that was a good thing, as it meant people were following the Lockdown rules and only key workers were making essential journeys. I felt proud to be helping get those key workers to where they needed to be to carry out essential jobs. On the other hand, it felt lonely on the quiet trains which are usually a busy, bustling environment.

One day, I was walking through an empty carriage and started singing the song 'All By Myself' in my head. It gave me an idea that I thought would be fun and might bring some smiles to people's faces. So, I set about filming my own lip-sync video, recreating a funny version of Céline Dion's 'All By Myself' music video onboard the train and on the empty platforms. I put the video on my own social media, then LNER asked if it could be shared on its social media channels too. From there, it went viral and thousands of people have since watched it. I hope it helped cheer people up during the pandemic.

As well as being a Train Manager with LNER, I volunteer as an emergency response driver, something I have been doing for five or six years. During the pandemic, I volunteered for extra shifts at BloodFast on days off from my railway job, helping to transport urgently needed medical items to hospitals around the UK. This includes blood, vaccines, doctors' notes, baby milk and more. It feels great knowing that I've helped people, and I really enjoy the driving too!

Looking forward, I think that with time life will go back to 'normal' eventually. People are having their vaccines and most people are following social distancing rules, which will all help normality to return. I do feel that some of our habits might change. For example, maybe we will start wearing masks whenever we have a cough or cold, to help reduce the spread of germs to other people.

It will be lovely to be able to meet family and friends again and have fun. I look forward to people being able to return to our trains for fun days out and to visit all the amazing places the UK has to offer, and everyone at LNER is working really hard to make sure people travelling with us stay safe.

Davey G

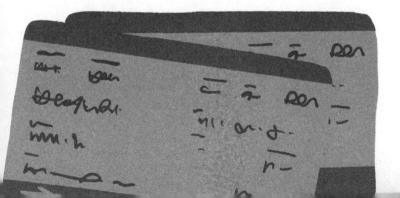

TESSA MATTHOLIE BUTUNOI

Global public health specialist and mum of two

Dear Arlo and Kika,

At the beginning of 2020 when COVID emerged, we were living in Nairobi, Kenya. I was working there for the UK government, for the Department for International Development (or DFID), in public health. I was living there with my husband George and our son Luci (who was three at the time) and I was pregnant with our second baby. On the 24th March 2020 we were given three days' notice that we going to be mandatorily evacuated and on Friday, 27th March we found ourselves on a plane back to the UK.

This was hard for all of us — we could only take what would fit in five bags and did not know how long we'd be going for, or if we'd be returning to Kenya. As things turned out, we never did. My son Luci had to leave behind his school, his friends, his home, and our beloved cat Slinks (Slinky Joe). Plus, I was 12 weeks pregnant and feeling sick as a dog. It was an incredibly stressful few days.

However, as soon as we were on the special BA flight and leaving behind the empty airport in Kenya, things started to settle. It was quite reassuring to be back in the UK, despite the weird times and empty roads. We had to drive all the way from the airport to Cornwall, which is where my family are based, with special letters from the government explaining why we had permission to travel, should anyone have stopped us to ask why we were out and about.

Summer 2020 was a weird and nomadic time with highs and lows. There was quite a lot of stress and uncertainty, particularly given the pregnancy. We stayed partly in rented accommodation (when it was available) and partly with family (when it wasn't), waiting until we could get back to Bristol. I had to essentially 'dock into' two different maternity care services (in Plymouth and Bristol) as we had no idea where we would be when baby number two decided to make an appearance. But there were also silver linings to this weird existence; we got to spend lots of extra time with family and on Cornish beaches, which would not have been possible had we stayed in Kenya.

As it happened, baby number two, Sebi, was born in Plymouth the night before we were supposed to move back to Bristol. He clearly could not wait as he was three weeks early. Loading all the bags into the car probably had something to do with it. . . I am just grateful that Sebi arrived safely. Oh, and we managed to eventually ship our cat and all our stuff back too and are now busy trying to plot our return to Africa with our boys!

Yours sincerely,

Tessa

Margaret (Maggie) Keenan

The first person in the world vaccinated against COVID-19 (outside of clinical trials) at University Hospital, Coventry

Dear Arlo and Kika,

Thank you for your lovely letter. Getting the vaccination came as a surprise to me. I was taken to hospital quite ill with a heart condition but thank God, I responded well to treatment and the care I received from the wonderful staff at the University Hospital, Coventry. I could not be more grateful.

I was asked if I'd have the vaccination – not thinking I was the world's first. I was nervous, excited and happy at setting an example and hoping I encouraged others to have it.

It was a massive day for me and millions of others as we look to get back to some kind of normality. Everything went by in a blur and it was surreal to see my name and pictures on the news and in the papers. Someone told me I was the number one trend in the world on social media and I couldn't believe it! I just feel really honoured to have had it done, to have been the first and to have got the ball rolling. I'm not sure it will ever truly sink in.

The first Lockdown was good because I have family living close. They did my shopping. My grandchildren came on their bikes, sat on the garden wall and I sat in the hall. We sang crazy songs and I told silly jokes. The second Lockdown was different because it was cold. I kept busy sewing, reading, and writing letters.

I do feel positive towards the future, and I'm sure things will be better. We have to make every day a happy one and keep smiling.

I wish you both good luck with your book. I am sure your parents and friends are very proud of you.

My very best wishes,

Maggie

NICOLA ADAMS OBE
Former professional boxer and
double Olympic champion

Dear Arlo and Kika,

Thank you so much for your letter, I really enjoyed reading it. I love the idea behind this and can't wait to read the collection. What a great way to make something beautiful out of a hard experience!

I am writing this on the anniversary of Lockdown, and though it's been an incredibly difficult time for everyone, I am trying to reflect on the positive things that I have achieved.

I've been lucky enough to work on several important projects during the pandemic. In 2020 I took part in Strictly Come Dancing which had always been a dream of mine (I'm glad you enjoyed watching it!)

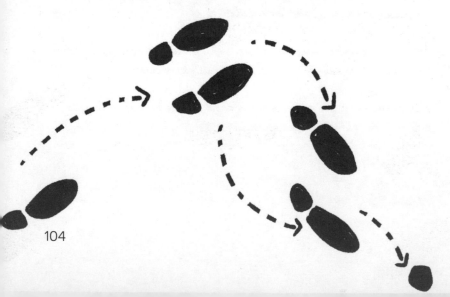

I wanted to demonstrate to people that I could do more than box, and, along with Katya Jones I was part of the first same-sex pairing in the show's history. I believe it's so important for people in the younger generation like you to see inclusivity on TV, and I feel proud to have been part of such an important milestone.

In terms of keeping myself busy, I have spent a lot of time working out. Fitness has always been a great release of energy for me, and I think that the pandemic has shown us how important exercise is for our mental health. It's been fantastic to see so many young people taking up exercise, such as in Joe Wicks' PE classes.

Although it's been incredibly difficult, particularly for BAME communities, who were hit particularly hard by the pandemic, Lockdown has given us all time to reflect on what's important. As the world was plunged into a collective experience, we realised that we are all, in the end, part of the same human race. Moments of real solidarity were born out of this feeling.

All the best,

Nicola

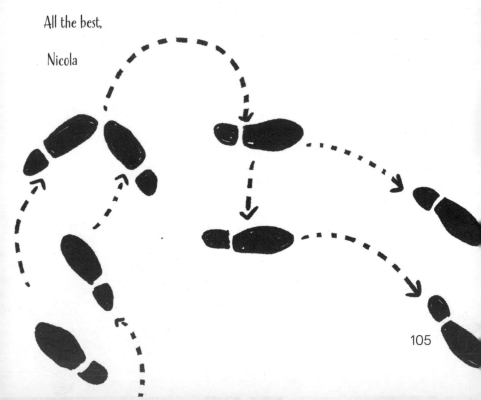

FOOD

RAYMOND BLANC OBE

Chef Patron at Le Manoir aux Quat'Saisons.
Author. Founder of Brasserie Blanc

Dear Arlo and Kika,

I was touched to receive your letter and wish you all the best with your book.

In fact, at the beginning of the pandemic I was embarking on my own book. My story of the pandemic is entwined within the story of that book. The two of them go together: salt and pepper, fish and chips.

I had wanted to write a book that would be a tribute to my mother and her cooking. I grew up in Franche-Comté, a region of France, and my childhood was spent playing in the forests that surrounded my home.

Everything we ate was grown locally, and dictated by the seasons. I helped my father in the garden, growing the vegetables, and Maman ruled the kitchen, and an excellent cook she was, too. She was a tiny woman with a hungry family of seven to feed. And was a huge influence on my career as a chef. We spoke every day on the phone.

As I say, I began work on the book. Then came Lockdown. While so much of my life had been spent in a professional kitchen, I was now at home. More and more, I found myself craving the food of my childhood.

Food and recipes are a connection to the people we love. One day, when you have left home, you will crave the dishes that take you back there. I dreamt of Maman's tomato salad and her vegetable and chervil soup, and of steak, fried in the pan, the way she made it with a little water added to the hot pan to create a tasty jus. I craved her apple tart, an omelette of Comté cheese, and the onion and bacon tart which, as a child, I adored. Of course, I made them all. As I cooked and ate, I was taken back to the past. With each meal, I was coming up with recipes for my little cookbook, 'Simply Raymond'.

We were a few months into Lockdown when I received a call from France. It was very sad news. Maman had passed away. She was in her nineties and had been unwell. Still, I was deeply shocked by the loss.

There have been few meals when I have not thought of her. Cooking brings us close together, even when we are not at the same table. Such wonderful memories of my mum are evoked by a mouthful of this or that, and then I smile at the memory of her smile.

I was reaching the end of my little book when I developed a cough. Soon I was feverish and next I was in hospital. Yes, I had Coronavirus. I stayed in hospital for four weeks. I am so grateful to the doctors and nurses of the NHS. Without them I might not be here to tell you this story. People ask me, 'Raymond, what did you make of the hospital food?' I fell in love with the custard: rich and velvety.

As for the future, I learnt to meditate in hospital and that was my saviour. I am changing my life, making improvements. What was once undervalued has become greatly valued. I am excited about the positive impact on our food culture; that we focus on a greener planet and sustainability, reconnecting with our farming and craftmanship.

This is the story of my Lockdown. Thank you for listening and I wish you good health and bon appétit.

With my best wishes,

Raymond Blanc

WILL SHU
CEO of Deliveroo

Dear Arlo and Kika,

Without a doubt, the past year has been one of the most unusual and challenging any of us have experienced. Every single person, from children to teachers to parents, has been affected by the pandemic, and it is no different for all of us at Deliveroo.

At Deliveroo, we work hard to make sure that tasty food is delivered straight to people's homes in the UK and around the world, and we love connecting people with wonderful restaurants in their local area.

None of this could be possible without Deliveroo's amazing riders who are at the heart of the business and make sure that people receive the food they need and want.

While our service provides joy and a treat to people at mealtimes, it quickly turned into a necessity over the past year, and we were so pleased to see riders given 'key worker status' — delivering an invaluable service to local communities across the UK, particularly the vulnerable and the elderly.

Overnight we had a responsibility to support those who were isolating at home and who were unable to leave their house.

We therefore decided to adapt our service to allow people to order from supermarkets and pharmacies to make sure they could still get the essential items they needed.

It is here that our incredible riders and restaurant partners played such an important role and we made it our absolute priority to support them as they supported others.

Our restaurant partners, grocers and riders have undoubtedly shown themselves to be heroes throughout this crisis. They have shown incredible strength as they work so hard to support and care for their communities. They continue to be a genuine inspiration to me.

Like the fantastic Simon Bucknell, a Deliveroo rider who tirelessly worked as an NHS volunteer during the pandemic, delivering food to NHS hospitals. There's also the brilliant Aja Aguirre, who raised £1,000 for the NHS with her football team, Nottingham Forest.

Other riders worked to support their local communities, and even ones further afield. One wonderful rider, Suhail Javaid, went above and beyond by donating his hard-earned money towards projects that provide food packs in Pakistan.

Countless other riders worked as doctors, were part of COVID-19 response units, or participated in everyday acts of kindness by helping get people groceries for free.

Our restaurant partners also worked day and night to keep their communities supplied with fresh food, and make sure they had enough to eat, such as 'Chicken and Blues' who gave NHS staff 50% off their menu. I could also name countless other heroic partners, and of course those who donated free food to our NHS campaign, such as Pizza Hut and Dishoom. Together we delivered 1 million free meals to hundreds of hospitals across the UK.

Reflecting on all the good our community can achieve makes me feel so positive about the future. This year has shown the public just how incredible our riders and restaurant partners are, and how willing they are to go the extra mile to support their loved ones and the wider community.

From all of us at Deliveroo, thank you!

Best wishes,

Will

GEORGE ALAGIAH OBE

BBC journalist and author

Dear Arlo and Kika,

Of all the Lockdown restrictions, the shared
experience of eating together is the one I
miss most. It's so much a part of my Sri Lankan
heritage. This goes back a long way to a childhood
in which food – the making of it and the sharing
of it – played such a central part in our lives.
I would watch my mother, typical of so many Sri
Lankan women of her generation, grinding the
spices, grating a coconut, stirring and tasting
until everything was just right. This was her
gift. And as my sisters and I grew up we, in
our turn, learnt that cooking could be a way of
showing our affection for each other and our
friends. So when this is all over we are going to
have a huge cook-in. What a feast we will have!

The pandemic presented special challenges for me and thousands of others who are cancer patients with ongoing treatment. But there was one way in which I felt I had an advantage. To have cancer is to live with uncertainty. Every scan brings with it a huge question mark over my life. So, I've learnt to live in the moment; to be content with today. It has helped me get through these most unpredictable of times.

As a foreign correspondent for much of my professional life I spent many years reporting on the lives of people less fortunate than those of us who live in the UK. The pandemic has eroded the gains of recent years, pushing tens of millions around the world back into poverty. And they are being left further behind in the vaccine rollout – only a tiny fraction of the doses delivered so far have gone to poorer countries, less than two per cent.

This pandemic has taught us that we need each other. That's what being human is – caring for one another, not just here at home but across the world. The word 'ubuntu' in the Zulu language sums it up. It means something like this: I am not human unless I recognise the humanity in others. It should be our motto as we emerge from this pandemic.

George x

John Vincent MBE

Entrepreneur and Co-Founder of
LEON Restaurants

Dear Arlo and Kika,

Thank you for the loveliest, most colourful letter I have received in a long time. Well done for 'trying not to argue', I am sure many people will understand that sentiment.

You asked what Lockdown has been like for me. Well, it has been like being in a COVID tumble dryer. You know when you watch your clothes going round and round? Sometimes stopping, not knowing when it is going to start again. Sometimes being left upside down, with all your money falling out of your pockets?

The business I started and run (LEON) has stayed open but we have lost lots of business so that has been hard. And lots of people have lost their jobs in the hospitality industry. I have done my best to try and keep people's morale up but many people are understandably sad that their restaurants have been shut for so long.

The biggest thing I am proud of during Lockdown is the work we did for FeedNHS. It became clear that because we were the only restaurant(s) that stayed open in Lockdown, the nurses and doctors were relying on us for food – and that

many intensive care workers were
unable to take breaks or leave the hospital. So, with
Damian Lewis (cool actor), Helen McCrory (cool actor too), Matt Lucas
(funny actor) and my team at LEON we raised enough money to
serve 1 Million meals to medical teams who really needed it.

LEON teams (and those of the other restaurant chains who re-opened some
of their outlets to help) got up early each morning and travelled across an
empty London to spend their days making as many meals as they could. We
received so many letters and emails from the wonderful people working in the
COVID wards.

I am looking forward to being let out of the COVID tumble dryer. It is still
stopping and starting, but when I am let out, I am going to hug my friends
and jump up and down with them at concerts. We have missed our daughter
Natasha who has been stuck abroad but have been lucky to be with Eleanor
our other daughter, who has been (not?) doing GCSEs (she seems to be studying
Snapchat).

Most importantly, Lockdown has taught me to tell my wife and my mum that I
love them more often. They have needed their own support but given so much
to me. Perhaps COVID has taught us all to remember what is important.

John x

MONICA GALETTI
Chef. Author. TV presenter

Dear Arlo and Kika,

Lockdown for me has been a mixed bag of emotions. I believe like a lot of people. Normally I am very busy with managing my restaurant Mere in Charlotte Street, London; filming, travelling and of course with family to balance.

With Lockdown it was lovely to have so much time with my family. It was difficult to adjust to staying at home every day but slowly we found a routine and lots of DIY projects to keep us occupied. It's been really special to be home for family meals more than once a week! Like the whole country we also have really missed seeing our friends, family and for us in particular all our team at Mere.

The first Lockdown was helped by the good weather we had and getting to spend more time enjoying and working in the garden.

Currently we are in our third Lockdown — being winter has made it feel so much longer but I'm still enjoying the family time. We are so looking forward to May when we will be able to open our restaurant again with our team and welcome back our guests. Fingers crossed things will continue to get better!

Yours sincerely,

Monica

TIM STEINER OBE
CEO of Ocado

Dear Arlo and Kika,

Britain's grocers bore a very heavy responsibility through the crisis to ensure that everyone, especially the most vulnerable, had safe and reliable access to food. This is our story.

On the March evening when the Prime Minister announced Lockdown, we had so many visits to Ocado.com that we thought it was a cyber-attack. Almost overnight, millions of people who would have normally gone to their local supermarket wanted to buy their groceries online. This meant making changes so we could meet the needs of our customers, including those most vulnerable.

Our software engineers worked around the clock to manage the traffic to our website and we even removed products that take up a lot of space in our vans, like bottled water and flowers, so we could deliver to more people. We kept reassuring people that there was more than enough food (and loo roll!) to go around.

I would like to pay tribute to the remarkable work of my colleagues in exceptional circumstances. We have shown, through extraordinary creativity, problem-solving, resilience and adaptability that technology can help us deliver food in the safest, most reliable, and most environmentally friendly way. As a result, we delivered more groceries to households than ever before and in the four weeks following the start of Lockdown we delivered more than 50 million items.

To keep people safe, we delivered orders to customers' doorsteps rather than bringing them into the kitchen and temporarily suspended taking back plastic bags for recycling. We made sure to provide our Customer Service Team Members — the wonderful people who do the deliveries — with the necessary personal protection equipment and regular COVID testing.

The world has changed. Millions of people have tried online grocery shopping for the first time, and we think they won't be going back. As a result, the landscape for food retailing is changing, for the good, and we're excited to be a part of it.

Yours sincerely,

Tim

COMMUNITY

GILL EDWARDS

Yorkshire bookseller. Purveyor
of imagination, knowledge and
dreams at The Little Ripon Bookshop

Dear Arlo and Kika,

Imagine you are in the middle of an amazing dream – perhaps you're
riding a glorious unicorn across a perfect blue sky or you're about to
score a winning goal – when SUDDENLY (and rather rudely) someone
tells you to PUT YOUR DREAM DOWN and get some sleep.

Well, there I am in March 2020, running my dream bookshop, when
suddenly I'm told to close the doors, pull down the shutters and wait
for a signal. How weird!

My job is to sell books – to match the right book to the right person.
'Let's see, you're 1.3 metres tall, you have size 3 feet and two scabs on
your knee – I think this book will be perfect for you!' I love it, and
when I'm told that I can't do it, I want to do it even more.

We spent the first week of Lockdown decorating our windows to cheer
people up. We had just run a World Book Day competition to decorate
loo rolls as book characters, so we made a fabulous gallery of about 100
of these hilarious little works of art to make passers-by laugh.

Then we set about adapting our business to cope with the situation. We spruced up our website, found new ways to take orders, and delivered books to our customers. We walked miles around the city to leave books on doorsteps, we drove round the Yorkshire Dales delivering to schools, farms and cottages, we rode a fleet of sky-pirate ships to here, there and beyond and popped paperbacks down chimneys (ok, we didn't do that last one but we have big ambitions!).

Books are important to people in times of crisis and, although my job is not nearly as important as many other jobs, I felt like I could carry on talking to people on the phone or by email, to let them know that we could still help them. We delivered birthday books to grandchildren and cheer-up books to lonely grandparents. We started Book Monkeys, our children's book club, on Zoom so we could keep chatting about books. Our annual Great Big Book Hullabaloo went online and reached even more schools. We filmed ourselves chatting about new books for school book fairs and Cressida Cowell joined us for our first virtual event!

Oh, and we did some cleaning and painting, so the shop was super shiny when we opened again!

It's been a challenge, but we've learnt that our business can change and survive and we're ready for anything. I think the future looks rosy and, of course, booky!

Gill Edwards

MAFF POTTS
Director, Association of Camerados

Dear Arlo and Kika,

Thank you for writing to me and asking me to be part of your brilliant project. Emails wither, letters endure. If I wore a hat, I would take it off to you, bravo.

My job is supporting something called Camerados, a movement of people all over the UK and the world who make places called public living rooms — a face-to-face space in your neighbourhood where you can go if you're having a rough day. Unlike most scary places we go in a crisis — police stations, hospital etcs — these places have fairy lights, sofas and normally some excellent biscuits.

When the pandemic hit, every one of the public living rooms had to close. Then a Camerado in Berlin got in touch with us and said she'd help us create a public living room that was online. We call it #SpoonRoom. Strangers come on a Zoom call with a spoon, and in groups of four each person gets three uninterrupted minutes to talk about our week and then we chat and wave our spoon when we want to say something. Some bring a teaspoon if they're feeling low or a spaghetti spoon if they're feeling great. My team hosts them twice a week but Camerados hosts them in Portugal, Germany, USA and New Zealand too. We've got each other through some tough times, with tears, laughter, and often a lot of both.

One day a woman called Paula joined, sitting in the dark. It turned out she had no money to pay for electricity but had enough power on her tablet to join SpoonRoom and she wasn't going to miss it. THAT is how important company is to people. Another person called Cal joins every week from the 9th floor of a council tower block in Newcastle. He is a hermit, living a very solitary life. His only friend, Clive, lived in the opposite block of flats and every night they would turn their lights on and off to say 'Goodnight' to each other. Clive died due to COVID and Cal has been struggling ever since.

My hope for the future is that we remember people like Paula and Cal when we rebuild the world after the pandemic. There are lots of people like them out there – the pandemic has given all of us a glimpse into what their life is like.

We can make a difference, because people have realised they have the power to look out for each other. What if we harness this energy for the future?

Every week I see people with bottomless sadness come together and leave one hour later laughing and singing and remembering the good things about being human. People are great, we just forget it sometimes. Maybe the pandemic has reminded us.

Good luck with your project, it is BRILLIANT and so are you,

Your Camerado,

Maff

Sir Keir Starmer MP
Leader of the Labour Party

Dear Arlo and Kika,

When Lockdown was first announced, I was in the final weeks of my campaign to become Leader of the Labour Party. My team, like so many others, had to quickly switch to working from home. One day we were meeting people face to face — the next we were stuck behind our computer screens.

In April, I became the first Labour leader to make my inaugural speech over video from my living room rather than to a packed hall of Labour supporters. Little did any of us know then that a year later so many of our lives would still be like this. We've had to adapt to a whole new way of working — and that has put all our technical skills to the test. Politicians aren't always the most tech savvy and it's fair to say the mute button has taken some getting used to.

I have spent more time at home than I have in years, including long evenings with my family in the garden instead of commuting. I noticed that a real sense of togetherness grew in communities up and down the country as people checked on neighbours and volunteered. There was entrepreneurship too. Walking down my high street one day, I popped by a local café which was selling masses of flour — as the country became obsessed with baking banana bread, they had spotted the business opportunity.

But the pandemic has revealed massive inequalities as well. There were so many who put their lives on the line to tackle Coronavirus. Not just health and social care workers, but also shop workers and bus drivers; the latter were far more likely to contract the virus and three times more likely to die from it. Three million people were excluded from support. Many have had to choose between their health and their livelihood. We must ensure that never happens again.

For me, the pandemic laid bare how unequal and unjust our society is. As we look towards the future, when Coronavirus no longer plays such a fundamental role in our lives, I hope we take the opportunity to stop and to focus on what sort of society we want to be in future.

Keir

JACQUIE JENKINS
Owner of The Hair Studio,
Llantwit Major, Wales

Dear Arlo and Kika,

My name is Jacquie and I run a hairdressing salon
in a little town called Llantwit Major in South Wales.

In March 2020 when we knew the cases of COVID were
rising, it was difficult to stop our elderly clients coming into
the salon to have 'one more hairdo' so they looked smart for
Lockdown!

I decided to close the salon, before the official Lockdown
was announced, to keep my staff and clients safe.

Clients have been so kind and thoughtful by buying vouchers
and paying in advance for their future haircuts to help us.
Some even paid for a whole year's worth of hair dos! I have
been really touched by people's kindness and the wonderful
community we live in.

For many clients, especially those who live on their
own, having their hair done is so much more than the
actual hairdo. They like the routine of their regular hair
appointment, it makes them feel good, they love the company,
and for some we may be the only people they have spoken to
for a while. I knew Lockdown would be difficult for them.

During Lockdown my staff and I rang our clients who live alone, just for a chat to see how they were doing and if they needed anything. They loved this and we loved keeping in touch with them.

I kept busy with gardening and I even grew some vegetables in pots for the first time. I also started running, something I never thought I would do!

I had mixed emotions about reopening after this latest Lockdown — apprehensive knowing how hard it was with all the cleaning, sanitising, wearing the masks and visors, but at the same time excited about getting back to seeing all our clients and working with my wonderful team. We have all missed each other!

Some clients were quite emotional when we rang them to let them know we were reopening, some even burst into tears! They have loved coming back in and have left with a spring in their step and smile on their face.

We have had lovely cards, messages, flowers, chocolates and gifts to welcome us back from our clients and that in turn has made me quite emotional.

COVID has been challenging in many ways but what it has highlighted to me is how vital social contact is for so many of our clients and how we as a salon play an important role in that.

Best wishes,
        Jacquie x

MARIE BENTON
Founder and Chief Executive,
The Choir With No Name

Dear Arlo and Kika,

My organisation, the Choir with No Name, runs choirs across England for people who have experienced homelessness. Before Lockdown, our choirs would meet every week to sing uplifting music and then sit down to a delicious meal together. It's a simple formula, but the power of singing your heart out among good friends has proved time and again to be a total winner in helping our members turn their lives around. For many, the beautiful choir community becomes a family, where a traditional family might not exist.

When Lockdown happened, like all separated families, we couldn't be together. But we were determined not to let that divide us! Our amazing teams of volunteers formed phone rotas and we called everyone regularly. We checked everyone had access to food, somewhere to stay, could get to their healthcare appointments, all that sort of thing. For our most isolated people, we turned up on their doorstep to serenade them! We also moved rehearsals on to Zoom, but many of our choir members weren't able to access them, either because they didn't have a smartphone or tablet, or because they didn't have the skills. So we also distributed a load of tablets, which our more digitally skilled choir members used to help their friends to get online. We also met in person when restrictions allowed, singing in parks and town squares and meeting in smaller groups where necessary.

One of our Liverpool choir members said this:

'This year has been very challenging for me. I lost my father in January, a friend/ex-partner in February, and my mother in October. The pandemic happening on top of all that has felt like a lot to deal with. The Choir with No Name has felt more like a family to me than ever and has helped me to not feel alone and overwhelmed by everything that has been happening. We are all helping each other through this difficult and challenging time, which warms my heart and gives me hope.'

We are all VERY EXCITED about getting together to sing again, and also looking forward to when we can perform to an audience once more! I know that it'll be some years before we fully understand the repercussions of the pandemic, and there will be hard times to come, but if we can all pull together and support each other as our choir members do then we will get through it.

I wish you the absolute best with your book and fundraising. I'm looking forward to hearing what all the different people you've asked have to say. Thank you for inviting me to be a small part of what I'm sure will be an important record of one of the craziest years in history.

With my warmest wishes,

Marie

MR HAPPY

Mr Men. Happiest person in the
land. Eternal optimist who can
even make a worm smile

Dear Arlo and Kika,

Have you ever heard of Happyland? On the other side of the world, where the sun shines hotter than here, there is a country called Happyland. Everybody who lives in Happyland is usually as happy as the day is long, but this last year has been a very different time. The flowers started to droop and you couldn't see smiling faces all around as everybody was wearing a mask. But I'm not called Mr Happy for nothing!

I live in a small cottage beside a lake at the foot of the mountain. The cottage has felt smaller than normal lately, but I've been enjoying lots more time walking in the woods near my home. I've noticed that Mr Busy isn't rushing around so much and Little Miss Splendid isn't buying so many new things! It's also not just Little Miss Chatterbox who wants to talk, but Mr Quiet and Little Miss Shy appreciate talking more too.

I think Happyland will come out of Lockdown an even happier place, with us knowing what's really important to us. When the masks are off, the smiles will be brighter than ever before!

I wish you could visit Happyland as it really is a very special place. But I think any place can be Happyland if you work together to make it that.

Wishing you much happiness,

Mr Happy

ELLIOT JACOBS

Postmaster, running a number of
stationery stores and Post Offices in
North London and Hertfordshire.

Dear Arlo and Kika,

Thank you so much for your wonderful letter. I
love receiving post - I expect that's why I love
my job as a Postmaster, running Post Offices in my
local area.

The Coronavirus pandemic has been so hard on
everyone and affected people in many ways - and
I'm glad to hear you're trying not to argue whilst
you are home schooling! That's not easy.

My Post Offices share the same shops as my
stationery company and both the stationery bit
and the Post Office have been open right through
the pandemic and we've seen lots of customers come
in really worried about what's going on. It's been
a real privilege to help people send letters and
parcels to loved ones when they can't see them
in person, as well as paying important bills, get
some cash for essential shopping, and maybe most
importantly - providing a friendly face for people
who might not have seen anyone for weeks.

My team and I have had to be careful going to work every day and serving customers, as there's lots to think about to keep us and our customers safe. That's why it's made me feel so sad when customers treat us badly. We've been called some horrible names and dealt with some really rude people who are frustrated by the situation – it's hurtful when we're just trying our best to help. But we've also had some lovely customers bring us chocolates, cakes and cards and even a drawing of us working – those things really make a difference on the tough days!

I do feel positive about the future – in many ways the pandemic has brought out the best in people, from neighbours doing shopping for each other, to key workers keeping us safe while they do their job on the frontline. We've all had a part to play and it shows what we can achieve together when we work as a community. I know some of my fellow Postmasters have even been honoured by the Queen for the work they have done supporting their local community, it's amazing to be a part of something so special.

I hope you've had lots of letters and we can raise lots of money for charity with your brilliant book. If you're ever passing one of my stores do pop in and say hello!

Until then,

Elliot Jacobs

Sir Trevor McDonald OBE

Newsreader and journalist

Dear Arlo and Kika,

I have found the Covid pandemic very long and very depressing. Most depressing has been the lack of any clear idea about when we might get back to normal. The experts are great but can't fully know how the virus might spread in the future.

So, I read a lot, watch too much television and when I talk to friends we seem to go over the same subject over and over again.

I miss seeing people and when I do, I am quite exhausted. The best thing is the growing sense of community. People appear more kind and concerned about the welfare of others. My neighbours have offered to help me shop. I don't need that help but it's wonderful to be asked. I do look forward to the end of it all and hope that we can soon return to normal.

Warm regards,

Trevor McDonald

TIM PEAKE
Astronaut. Pilot. Author

Dear Arlo and Kika,

Thank you for your lovely letter. It sounds like you have been incredibly busy during Lockdown and well done on creating such a wonderful project for an important charity. Thank you for what you are doing to help others.

In some ways, life in Lockdown is like living on the International Space Station. Your home becomes your place of work, you're cut off from people you care about and life can be more stressful than normal. Admittedly, the food is way better at home and I get to spend time with my wife Rebecca and our two boys! I can also go outside to exercise, which is something I really missed whilst in space. The view of Earth from space is so incredibly beautiful, but nothing beats actually being on Earth and surrounded by nature — something that we can often take for granted.

Sometimes when we feel overwhelmed by circumstances that are beyond our control, I find it really helps to focus on the things that you CAN control. That might be planning how you'll spend your day, where you can go for exercise or who you will call and chat to. My boys enjoy art and sharing their pictures with family and friends. Finding something, even a small thing, that will bring some happiness to your day and to someone else's can really give your mood a boost.

Our world is full of kind, determined, talented and brave young people who will be the positive change makers of our future and now we will need them more than ever. However, I also want them to know they have grown-ups who believe in them and the amazing things they are capable of and that we'll be supporting and helping them all the way. I am definitely optimistic about the future — I've seen what amazing things we can achieve when we work together.

Keep up the great work and remember to look up at the stars!

Tim Peake

AT HOME

MALALA YOUSAFZAI
Activist for female education. Nobel
Prize Laureate

Dear Arlo and Kika,

Thank you so much for your kind letter.

I know that life can feel frustrating and frightening during this pandemic. Even though our daily lives look very different now, it is important to focus on things we can do, like following safety guidelines, helping others and keeping our minds active.

I've been trying to learn some new skills at home. I'm taking Swahili classes and learning to code. I've also read quite a few books.

Am I optimistic about the future? Absolutely! Young people like you two, and others I've met in many countries around the world, give me hope. In different ways, they are trying to make our communities better. Some are working on climate change to protect our planet. Others are making their schools safer. Others are fighting discrimination and racism. And there are many people like us making sure that girls have equal access to education. These children and young people know that you don't have to wait to be an adult to be a leader — and I'm so inspired by them.

Thank you very much for your letter, Arlo and Kika.

Malala

BRUNO TONIOLI
Entertainer

Dear Arlo and Kika,

Thank you for your letter. What a great idea.

I consider myself very lucky, and, yes, I did find things to busy myself.

I love gardening and I often found myself having heated conversations with my hibiscus plant! My neighbour thought I'd completely lost it, but the hibiscus loves it — it quadrupled its exotic blooms in a week!

News spread in my street about my miraculous plant powers, and I have since rescued four abandoned star jasmines and an assortment of succulents left in the recycling station with a very unhappy bougainvillea.

Emboldened by my success as the plant whisperer, I then decided to tackle my overgrown and tangled pomegranate tree. I got so overexcited with pruning that I reduced the tree to a skeletal bush. The poor thing lost all its leaves in shock. But I can now see vibrant new growth appearing — tough love bears fruits.

Keeping the house tidy is another thing that can keep you busy and fit. I embarked on a spring clean, starting with polishing all my wooden floors. Armed with a bucket of detergent and sponges, off I went. After four hours on my hands and knees I looked like a drowned rat on a chemical spill with painful blisters everywhere. But the floors were spotless.

One day I thought the Lockdown was the perfect opportunity to try something new, so I shaved my head. I called my agent on FaceTime looking like a murderer, suggesting my new look would be ideal for a role in the new Bond film or a Tarantino extravaganza. She suggested . . . 'EastEnders'. Very disappointing!

I exercise every day, but I tend to forget that I am no longer twenty. Though I can still manage a decent second position on the floor, the splits are out. I can manage 240 press ups per week, with breaks in between, and I continue to practice yoga poses (or asana, to be correct) — so good for mind and body. I must remind myself not to have a large breakfast before practice, as it can make the downward dog quite windy, and the reverse triangle on a full stomach could cause irreversible damage to your pride and underwear.

I look forward to performing and entertaining again, travelling, and seeing my friends in person.

In the meantime, keep strong in mind and body; read books; exercise as much as you can; keep in touch with friends and family; talk to someone every day.

Lots of love,
        Bruno Tonioli

RENE GERMAIN
Writer. Speaker. Creator of
BLK & GREAT

Dear Arlo and Kika,

How are you? It's been a pretty weird year, right?

My name is Rene and I am a Product Manager and writer.
As a Product Manager, I work with an amazing team to
build things that people will hopefully like and use again
and again. Alongside this, I'm writing a book called 'Black
and Great' which will feature successful black people talking
about their careers across a variety of industries, including
science, law, music, TV, technology and more. It's coming out
in August and I'm very excited. Before the Lockdown, I was
able to interview some of the people for my book in person
which was truly a dream.

Then the Lockdown was announced, and things rapidly
changed. I had to work from home which meant I didn't
get to see my colleagues any more and all the interviews for
my book had to be completed virtually. At first, I was ok
because I thought it would only last a few weeks, but then

the weeks turned to months. Every day felt the same (pretty boring) and even small things like going food shopping felt a little scary because everyone was wearing masks and we'd all have to wash our hands constantly because of the virus. Some days I felt happy and hopeful; other days I felt down because I didn't know when this would end. I had never seen anything like this in my life.

But it hasn't all been doom and gloom. Over the past year I've used the extra time at home to read more, learn about my hair and how best to look after it (I have tightly curled hair, which turns into a big afro when brushed out) and become a far more adventurous cook.

I've gained a newfound appreciation for the people in my life because I wouldn't have been able to stay so positive without them. My boyfriend and I celebrated our birthdays together, just the two of us, playing board games and inventing our own drinks; plus, my friends and I have become closer as we talk all the time now (although not in person).

Though the Lockdown hasn't been easy, it's just one example of many periods in our lives where something unexpected happens and we need to change how we do things. Change isn't necessarily a bad thing if we're able to seek out the positives. I now look back on this Lockdown period with a smile because I learnt so much about myself and the things that really matter to me.

I hope Lockdown has been manageable for you and that you are able to see the light at the end of the tunnel.

Rene Germain

ROMESH RANGANATHAN

Comedian. Presenter. Actor

Dear Arlo and Kika,

My initial feeling when the country went into Lockdown and schools closed was sympathy for our children. They were not able to see their friends, enjoy school and, worse than that, had to spend a lot of time with their parents, without distractions like theme parks and excursions.

I think a lot of people lost a sense of who they are during the pandemic. We attach so much of what we are to our jobs, and our social circles, and so when those were taken away you can understand why people found the mental processing of what has happened incredibly challenging.

There have been positives to take from it, though. My kids are obsessed with video games, which is something my wife and I had very much left them to get on with. Being stuck at home, however, we felt the best course of action was to join in. My wife and I have had a number of sessions of 'Fortnite' with the boys and, in the game, they end up taking the parental role and showing us where things are and giving us virtual medical

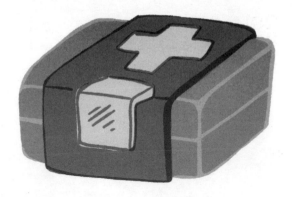

packs when we need them. It's sweet, and I very much enjoyed spending the games targeting and taking out my wife because she was the only one I could beat.

We have also spent time on walks as a family. This is something the boys have a short tolerance for, but when my wife commented on how much they were complaining I made the point that if three boys of their age DON'T find walking through some botanical gardens boring, that's the bigger issue.

We are excited about this all coming to an end of sorts. I can get back to live work, and my wife and children can get back to normality. My wife and I have expressed a sadness about losing the experience of spending all of our days together, and the children have very kindly pretended they agreed. I think that, looking forward, we will aim to set aside chunks of time to spend as a family, as we really have loved doing that. We have promised the boys we will limit the garden walks though.

Romesh

JAMES GRAHAM OBE

A writer of plays and TV dramas
and films

Dear Arlo and Kika,

It's quiet where I am. What does it sound like where you are? What can you hear right now?

Normally there are planes passing over my house, but there are none today. There weren't any yesterday, and I don't think there'll be any tomorrow.

I'm looking at my diary. Normally I might be going to a theatre to rehearse a play I have written, with actors and a director (I'm very lucky, normally, because this is always so much fun!). But my diary is empty today.

Theatre is the opposite of being in Lockdown, because what makes theatre so special is that you watch it all together, as a real community, in a physical space, sharing the same oxygen as the people performing the show. You laugh together, cry together, applaud together.

Normally.

But today I'm not experiencing any of that, I'm just looking at my phone. Normally there would be messages from friends about going somewhere this evening – to have a meal or go to the cinema or watch a play.

Normally . . .

It's OK, though. Do you know why?

Instead of the planes roaring overhead, I can hear the birds sing. I hardly ever noticed them before. Even though I know they were always there, competing with the noise of the non-stop city. So, I've started to learn their different tunes to get to know their names. Today I've heard a blackbird, a blue tit, a wood pigeon and a wren (I think. Please don't test me! I'm still learning.)

Instead of reading my diary, I'm reading a book, written by someone else, falling into another person's life. Instead of going somewhere to do something, my neighbours are handing a meal they have cooked over the fence for me to eat, and we'll talk. I hardly ever found time to speak to the people living right next door and along my street. I'm getting to know their names. There's Jon and Deborah, and Caroline, and Kevin. (I think. Please don't test me! I'm still learning.)

Instead . . .

Not 'normal'. But 'instead'. 'Instead' can be scary or strange. It's not always something you can control. Not regular, like planes; or familiar, like diaries; or escapist, like fun with friends. But it can be comforting, like birdsong; distracting, like books; and surprising, like the people next door.

It's OK to miss normal things when they're not there. But there'll always be other sounds and stories and surprises instead.

What have you learnt, where have you gone, who have you met instead? I can't wait to hear all about it . . .

James.

ROJA DOVE

Perfumer. Writer. Creator of Roja
Parfums

Dear Arlo and Kika,

Thank you for your letter. Here is what Lockdown meant to me.

Lockdown – A deadly plague – who would have guessed? People dying all around the world and lives in freefall. It sounds like a Hollywood disaster movie.

I will always remember walking into my favourite restaurant, The Wolseley on Piccadilly, and how the scent of hand-sanitizer overwhelmed the familiar and welcoming scents that usually greeted you.

Another, in April – the worst of the things happened as I lost my sense of smell. It was frightening, particularly because my job relies on my nose, but luckily within a month it returned and I started to fill my days in new ways. I had never spent so much time at home, as work always meant travel and time away. Suddenly I had time to spend in my garden and to rekindle my love of baking. Each week I looked forward to making scones, with strawberries and cream, and enjoyed them in the garden with my partner, Peter, and his close friends, sharing time together, whilst at the same time staying apart. It was an important lifeline – and so, weekly 'Tea and Scandal' was born.

The air was cleaner, and the smell of it clearer. The quiet allowed nature to flourish, and for us to reconnect with it. I certainly never remember hearing such a cacophony of birdsong. It was beautiful.

The world seemed to have slowed down, and people had time to be kinder – a smile, a hello, time to rediscover what being human meant. Hopefully, this is something that will stay with us, and the world will be a little bit kinder.

Roja Dove

Helena Bonham Carter CBE
Actress

Dear Arlo and Kika,

What a great and beautiful idea. I hope you raise lots and lots of money to help those who have really suffered during COVID.

I think one of the (silver linings) to this pandemic is how compassionate people have shown themselves to be. Everyone in the world has been affected in some way, everyone is aware, and people are really looking out for each other. Those three words that are often used automatically, 'How are you?' are asked with a meaning that they never had before.

The pandemic had been a thief to many while it has given things to others. But it so depends on your circumstances and time of life. This has been a time when I know I have truly tasted my luck. I have a home with enough space, and the people and dogs
 • I share it with are beings I love very much. I am also happy in my own skin. Which has not always been the case throughout my life!

Different decades need different things. I'm 54 and 3/4 and the most precious thing for me is TIME. I feel it goes too fast, except in Lockdown when suddenly I have had bags of it.

What I have I done with it?

Well, instead of whizzing around like a headless chicken trying to complete 'to do' lists, I have sometimes done NOTHING. I have had snoozes (I'm v good at that) when I want. I've read lots (and because I liked the cover of the book, not because I've had to for work). I did a bit of home improvement (half of my hallway is now pink ... have yet to finish ... again something I'm very good at: not finishing things). I've phoned friends in the middle of the day to chat.

One thing that happens when you are an actor is that when you don't have an acting job you can feel very paranoid that everyone else is acting away. But in Lockdown, all actors were in the same boat, not working. So hooray! A holiday from professional paranoia! It's so stupid how so often we put our own happiness in the hands of what others are or are not doing ...

Anyhow, I've rambled and meandered ... because it's Lockdown and I have the time. You asked what I feel about the future and I'd say very positive. I hope you do too. You haven't been able to do the things you are used to, but what you

have built is a superpower that
will last for the rest of your life.
Resilience. Don't underestimate that.

I think the ordinary things will taste super sweet
again. It often takes being deprived of something
to truly appreciate it. Once this pandemic is over
(and it WILL end - everything does) we will find
wonder from things we'd never experienced before.

Love Helena B.C

TAKING
ACTION

BENJIE AND GEORGIA INGRAM-MOORE

Grandchildren of Captain Sir Tom Moore

Dearest Arlo and Kika,

Wow! You have been busy.

Thank you both for your wonderful letter, we were absolutely delighted to receive it. You have done an amazing job with your fundraising and what a lovely way to do it. I am sure that everyone has enjoyed receiving your letter as much as us.

The pandemic and Lockdown have had a huge impact on our family. We lived at home quietly with our mum, dad and grandad, Captain Tom Moore, for thirteen years and little did we know what a sunny barbeque would end up becoming.

Grandad was recovering from a fall and was determined to get back to being mobile again (he had secretly bought himself a treadmill but that's another story).

So, as we all sat outside in the sun, our dad jokingly offered Grandad £1 for every lap he did of our garden path to see if he could make 100 laps before his 100th birthday.

Grandad was always determined and made it his mission to reach the 100 laps, particularly as we agreed the money would go towards the NHS COVID-19 appeal.

Then things accelerated. It was picked up by the local media and before long it was being shown around the world. The total amount he raised ended up being just under £40 million with donations from 163 countries.

Grandad always encouraged us to be brave, fear nothing and follow whatever path we wanted. He said never to think that anything is beyond your reach.

We are incredibly proud of him. He proved that it does not matter how old you are, adventures are just around the corner.

We miss him very, very much, but we can still hear his voice telling us to not be sad and to enjoy every moment in life.

He would be very impressed with what you are doing. He would be shouting, 'Great work Arlo and Kika! Look at what you've both achieved!'

Then he would probably offer you a big piece of his favourite Victoria sponge cake to celebrate.

Love,

Benjie and Georgia Ingram-Moore

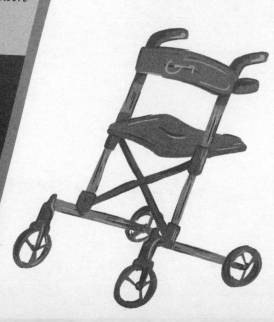

Dr Ali Joy

GP in London. Loves medicine's academic and diagnostic aspects. Keen contemporary art fan

Dear Arlo and Kika,

Thank you so much for your lovely letter.

The day I'm writing this is the anniversary of the first UK lockdown. I remember arriving home just in time to catch Boris Johnson's lockdown broadcast to the nation with our bubble of seven. Comparisons with wartime are inevitable – we were crowded round the TV in an atmosphere of camaraderie and concern.

As a doctor I had of course been following the Wuhan story. I was warning my patients in January and the death of Dr Li Wenliang on 6th February struck a chord. He was the hero who started the #CanYouManageDoYouUnderstand after he whistle blew in China. I was astonished by the complacency of our government and took to the media to express my outrage at the lack of testing, whilst the World Health Organization was saying 'test, test, test'.

I decided to do something. I explored which COVID tests were best, acquired as many as I could and then got into my red Mini, hazmat suit on, and set off! I went wherever I was needed to help people get tested. Your lovely parents even set up a tent decorated with flowers and fluffy sheep for a day of testing!

The lack of PPE for frontline health workers was shocking. In response, I started 'Covid Smart' with another concerned person, working to provide immediate help for these frontline workers. I raise the money and my partner sends out the parcels, organises the installation of washing facilities outside hospitals, and provides counselling to whoever puts in an urgent plea. We talk daily, though I still haven't met her as she lives in Manchester. I can only imagine what the fear of having inadequate PPE must be like. I volunteered to work in an NHS ICU and for 24hrs I shook with fear, but haven't felt fear since.

I learnt so much from testing. The two most concerning things were the clusters around restaurants, and so 'Eat Out to Help Out' would always contribute to a second wave; and that patients with mild illness often don't produce any or many antibodies — this showed how important T cell immunity is and how antibody levels may be misleading.

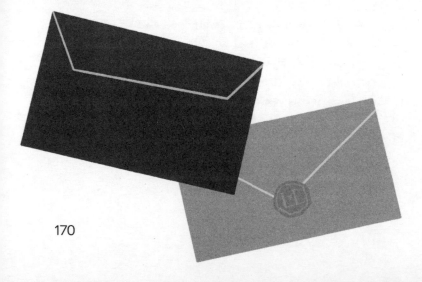

In August the rapid antigen lateral flow test appeared globally. I lobbied the government to give these to state schools so that children from the most disadvantaged homes could return to school, but the message fell on deaf ears, so I started doing these tests too. I hope it has helped hundreds to make safer decisions.

You two have wonderful parents as role models and I'm sure my advice to you is the same as theirs – if you see something that needs doing, do it!

Love,

Dr Ali

CHIMWEMWE CHIWEZA

Gender Studies student at the University of Malawi. Girl Up regional leader for Malawi. Co-Founder of Move Malawi Charity Organisation

Dear Arlo and Kika,

I remember the day like it was yesterday. It was March 20th and I was in class waiting for my lecturer, who was thirty minutes late. I study at the University of Malawi, Chancellor College in Zomba city, Malawi. (A little heads up – some college classes are just as exhausting as those back in primary school, or high school for that matter.) As we continued to wait for my delayed lecturer, a message sprang up on my phone. It was an official school message that read:

'TO ALL STUDENTS, please be advised that the President has declared a national state of emergency and all schools should be closed by the 24th of March.'

Everyone was immediately excited, as if they hadn't been dozing off just two minutes ago. To be honest, so was I and, c'mon, who wouldn't be? It sounded like a free holiday after all! Little did I know what was in store for me. The first few days were a blast as expected – sleeping late, waking up late, and no homework. But by day sixty, I was beginning to get tired of the never-ending routine so I decided to get productive. As the weeks rolled by, I started a small business selling donuts, participated in a seven-week feminist leadership course, and entered two essay writing competitions. I won one of them!

I was happy I wasn't just sitting around doing nothing. But it wasn't enough. People were dying every day because of COVID and I wanted to help. I sat down and thought about ways I could help my community. So, my Girl Up club and I identified a group of individuals who started a 'food for health workers' program and we volunteered with them as cooks. What struck me the most during the time we served was the dedication and selflessness of the health workers. They were probably working in the worst conditions I have ever seen our general hospital in, but that didn't stop them. They worked tirelessly to make sure lives were preserved. This made me think about the many times I never thought I could help or make a difference because I didn't have enough to offer. It made me realise that just giving your time to be there for someone in need makes all the difference.

It was seven months by the time the partial Lockdown was lifted. In those months I learnt that in tough times like the pandemic, there is power in looking on the bright side, never losing hope. It is in those times that you should choose to surround yourself with positive news and if you see a person around you who is feeling down or is in need of help, reach out. Never think you are too small to make a difference.

Lots of love,

Chimwemwe Chiweza.

Dear Arlo and Kika,

Thank you ever so much for your lovely letter, complete with exceptional handwriting skills and bold, decorative, coloured balls. Forgive me for typing my reply – my handwriting is as legible as a Harley Street doctor's and harder to decipher than the Enigma code.

What an inspired idea to write a letter a day during Lockdown. On hearing of your venture, I decided to attempt the same, but gave up with exhaustion on Day Three, after writing the letter 'C'.

I am also very impressed that you are doing this project together. Had I tried anything similar at your age with my older brother (who I love dearly), I'm quite sure one of us would have 'accidentally' pushed the other out of the window by now. Ground floor, of course.

How lovely that you live on a farm with lots of animals. How does that work? Who does the cooking?

I should imagine pigs find it hard to switch the
Aga on with those hooves. Mind you I am quite sure
a dolphin could do it. Dolphins are very clever,
apparently. I'm not sure dolphins are considered
a farm animal though, so I imagine you all have to
exist on cold food. I hope that doesn't get too dull.

In response to your question about how my life has
been affected in the pandemic, I was actually in
Chicago about to film a TV pilot when the pandemic
began and I was flown back to London (where I
live) after less than 48 hours. A TV pilot is a test
episode, in case you didn't know, so that the people
who run the TV channel can decide whether to make
a whole series of it or not. It could be that you
already know this, because your mother works in
television. If I remember rightly, she is a dancer
who won a newsreading competition.

Anyway, I returned to London and sat in my
little house and watched lots of people on the
news (ironically not your mum) failing to social
distance. Having taken delivery of a new piano
(I sensed I would be stuck at home for a bit and
thought it would be nice to use the time to improve
my playing) I was inspired to rewrite the words
to 'Thank You Baked Potato', a song I had written
and performed on television nearly twenty years
earlier. The new lyrics included some dos and don'ts
regarding safety during the pandemic. I recorded
myself warbling away and posted it on Twitter.

Well blow me down. It went viral and within days I had recorded the song in my bedroom and released it with all proceeds going to FeedNHS. This was a charity set up to provide healthy food for frontline workers in hospitals who were doing very long shifts on empty stomachs, as the supermarkets were empty.

As the song grew in popularity – reaching the top of the iTunes Chart and also the UK Download Chart – I began to record duets with lots of amazing people – Gary Barlow, Brian May, the English National Opera, the BBC Concert Orchestra, even some of my favourite Arsenal players joined in the fun. There was a 'Thank You Baked Potato' book and a cuddly toy, all raising more money for FeedNHS and I was very touched by how people responded. It felt like something good had come out of something bad.

After that I went to stay for nearly two months in a giant bubble to film my first series of 'The Great British Bake Off'! Not only was it very nice to eat lots of delicious cakes, but I also made new friends in Noel, Paul and Pru and the bakers and the crew who work so hard on the show. The only bit

I didn't like was when we had to say goodbye to a baker at the end of each episode. If it were up to me they'd all win. Also if no-one left each week, there would be more cakes to eat. See, there is a method in my madness.

I'm at home again now, writing a book and wondering what to do next with my friend Baked Potato. Hmmm.

I do feel positive for the future. I am looking forward to travelling again, and to spending time with family and friends, whom I miss terribly. One of my besties had his first baby - a beautiful girl called Rosa - nearly a year ago and I still haven't met her yet. I think when I finally do, I will probably burst into tears. I'm a soppy sausage at times.

Thank you again for your letter and I wish you all the very best and please give my love to the pigs and sheep and chickens and dolphins and elephants and pterodactyls and all the other animals on your farm.

Yours,

Matt Lucas (aged 47)

JOSIE NAUGHTON
Co-Founder and CEO of Choose Love

Dear Arlo and Kika,

Having spent five years working in the humanitarian sector as the Co-Founder & CEO of Choose Love, a non-profit organisation working to support refugees along the migration routes in Europe, the Middle East and the US-Mexico border, I rarely found myself at home in East London, but that all changed when the UK government announced the first Lockdown in March 2020.

Working from the tray table on a plane to suddenly the desk in my front room took some adjusting. I felt very disconnected from the world and concerned about how we were going to effectively fund our partners on the ground, who were having to find new ways to support tens of thousands of vulnerable people living in overcrowded refugee camps, unable to isolate when needed or easily access water, sanitiser, and PPE. Luckily, with our team located around the world and video conference

calling the new norm, we were quickly able to set up new lines of communications and continue our work.

As for many, the Lockdown has been an emotional rollercoaster, with good days and bad. However, one of the things I am most grateful for is the extra time to think and strategize. Even though there has been so much loss, we have also seen how incredible the human spirit is. I remember getting goosebumps and feeling very emotional as people of all ages came out of their homes to clap for the NHS. At the start of the summer, we managed to launch the 'Choose Our NHS' and 'Choose Our Carers' t-shirts for NHS Charities Together and The Care Workers Charity. The public was so supportive and helped us raise over £100k. I began to realise how resilient people could be and what great things could be achieved when we worked together as one humanity.

When the COVID-19 restrictions ease, I hope that the world doesn't go back to 'normal'. Instead, I hope we rebuild a world that is more equitable, just, and more deeply rooted in love and compassion. From many of the movements we have seen emerging in recent times, I really do feel this is possible.

With love,

Josie Naughton

Karl Jones
Sterile technician at Wockhardt UK

Dear Arlo and Kika,

I wanted to share with you my story of life during Lockdown.

My name is Karl, I am 30 years old. Today I am saving lives.

Before the pandemic I was an entertainer. I was a fire eater, juggler, balloon modeller and party event host extraordinaire. I was enjoying entertaining children just like you and your families. Once the pandemic took its grip my pipeline of parties, events and festivals dried up overnight. I no longer had any crowds, any bookings, or a job. It was a worrying and uncertain time and brought with it both money and career concerns.

That is until I applied for a role in a brand-new manufacturing project that proved to be the 'salvation of mankind' according to Prime Minister Boris Johnson.

I was fortunate enough to have heard about roles available as production line operatives at the COVID-19 fill-finish (the process of filling vaccine into vials) facility at Wockhardt

based in Wrexham. The firm had committed to a UK
government contract to produce as many vials of the Oxford
AstraZeneca vaccine as it could over an 18-month period and
the plant needed more employees to make this happen.

I joined more than 400 colleagues at Wockhardt who are
working towards stopping COVID-19 in its tracks by fill-
finishing vaccines for the UK's inoculation targets.

In my day-to-day role I help inspect the vials and pack them
into boxes ready for distribution to the NHS. I really enjoy my
work and have a huge sense of pride in what we are collectively
achieving as a group of people from all different backgrounds
here at Wockhardt.

Before the pandemic, I used to love seeing people smile and
wowing them with my skills. I think this role still allows me to
do that. I've gone from 'fire eating' to 'firefighting' and
am immensely proud of the little part I am playing in saving
the world.

Sending you all the best health,

Karl

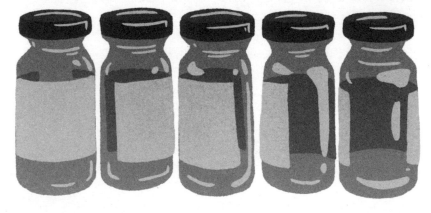

ROSIE MITCHELL
COVID-19 vaccinator, Sussex
Community NHS Foundation Trust

Dear Arlo and Kika,

I started working as a vaccinator for Sussex Community NHS Foundation Trust in December, months after taking redundancy from British Airways, where I'd worked as cabin crew for almost 25 years.

I didn't want to leave because it was part of my identity; but it was offering mixed flying — short and long flights — which wasn't suitable because I have two children. Henry and his twin sister, Mariella, made me feel better when they said, 'I'm so glad you don't do that job anymore, Mummy, because now I can see you every night!'

I didn't want to be stuck in front of a desk all day after leaving BA. I thought of joining the NHS but didn't think it was possible. Then I saw the advertisement for the vaccinator job. They were asking for cabin crew, in particular, because of our advanced first aid training.

I really wanted to be part of the effort to get everything back to normal. It's a bit like a war effort. Everyone is from different backgrounds and we are just pulling together. It's a really nice atmosphere.

It's very similar to BA: the hierarchy, camaraderie, making people feel welcome and at ease. It's about using my transferable skills — but not at 35,000ft!

I like the contact with patients, many of whom are so worked up by the time they get to me that they become overwhelmed by emotion. 'It's perfectly normal to feel like that,' I say.

My experience has improved my view of the NHS so much that I hope to continue working for it when the pandemic is over. The dedication and commitment of the staff is incredible. They are really professional and brilliant. We are really lucky to have people like that in the NHS.

Yours sincerely,

Rosie

A TIME
WITHOUT
TRAVEL

SIR ANDY MURRAY OBE

Professional tennis player.
Double Olympic gold medallist

Dear Arlo and Kika,

It was really nice to receive your letter and I'm glad you have been managing to do your schoolwork while the Lockdown has been going on. It's lucky you've also had some farm animals for company!

It's been a really tough time, everyone has been affected in one way or another, sadly with many people losing loved ones.

The frontline workers have been amazing, literally putting their lives on the line on a daily basis. This has made me feel really proud and has given me cause for optimism.

I've been at home for most of it, with the tennis tour being put on hold, so I, like most people, have become a part-time teacher (I have four young children at home), and it's definitely given me a new-found respect for the brilliant job teachers do. It's also highlighted how bad my art and craft skills really are (although I had my suspicions).

Instead of being out on the road competing, I've been able to spend extra time with my family, which is something I've loved. But I'm also very aware it's been a lot tougher for a lot of people.

I do feel optimistic about the future. This strange time has shown that there are so many heroes out there — NHS workers, emergency services, teachers, transport workers, volunteers — and that communities can come together to help each other out. I hope people can carry on looking out for others after the pandemic is over.

It's tough that you haven't been able to see your friends, but just think how excited you'll be when restrictions end. You'll certainly appreciate things like that a little bit more; I know I will.

Thanks again for writing and hopefully one day we can meet up.

Take care,

Andy

ROSIE JONES
Comedian. Actress. Author

Hello Arlo! Hello Kika!

My name is Rosie. I am a comedian and a writer. My Lockdown has been very up and down, like a daily rollercoaster!

Before the pandemic, I was VERY busy. As a comedian, I travel up and down the country, gigging in a different town every night. I lived out of a suitcase, and I only went home once every few weeks to pick up a fresh pair of pants.

I was even getting ready to travel abroad, and in March 2020 I was going to go to Australia for the Melbourne Comedy Festival — I was so excited! But Coronavirus stopped all of that, and overnight my diary completely emptied. For the first time ever, I had nothing to do.

To begin with, I was sad. I love my job very much; there's no better feeling than making people laugh.

But after a few weeks of feeling sorry for myself, I began to enjoy certain aspects of Lockdown. I realised that I may have been working a little too hard before, and I loved finally having evenings to myself. I went back to Yorkshire and stayed with my parents too. The three of us spent the year baking, walking, and watching loads of telly.

Every single Saturday I held a Zoom quiz for my friends too. I love writing quizzes and it was such a good way to keep in touch with pals who live in the UK and abroad. No matter how sad or boring my week had been, I always had Saturday's quiz to look forward to. Despite us all being thousands of miles apart from each other, we'd always have such a hoot!

I still worked too, of course, and I managed to write a children's book and do lots of online comedy gigs (which is essentially just me yelling jokes at my computer screen).

Now that Lockdown is easing slightly, I am very excited to get back to performing live comedy, and making people laugh away from my computer screen... bring it on!

Saying that, however, I don't think I'll be working as much as before. I will definitely be making lots more time for friends and quizzes!

Stay safe, and lots of love,

Rosie x

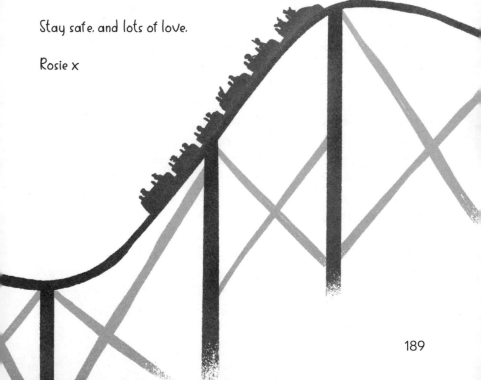

SOPHIE GONZALES
Australian Young Adult author

Dear Arlo and Kika,

When I was fourteen, I watched The Simpsons Movie for the first time. At the risk of spoiling a movie which, at the time of writing, is over a decade old, a big plot point follows a giant glass dome which is dropped over the town of Springfield, trapping its citizens — and the city's deadly pollution levels — inside, to protect the rest of the country. I had no way of knowing that, thirteen years later, I would be trapped inside a 'dome' of my own.

When Coronavirus hit Australia in March 2020, there was a sense that we were all in Lockdown together. But then the second wave hit in mid-June. This time, it only hit Victoria. My state.

Immediately, the rest of the country slammed their borders closed. We couldn't leave. For ANYTHING; danger, sickness, funerals. Nothing. They were on that side of the line. We were on ours. And on our side of the line, life was about to change.

We locked down hard for 112 days.

The rules were clear. You can only leave your house to exercise once per day. Only one person can buy groceries. If you leave your house, you must wear a mask (rumours spread about police officers stalking the streets, fining maskless people taking their bins to the curb). You cannot visit anyone, EVER. Luckily,

I'm a young adult author, so I could easily work from home (although, it's hard to write when you're starting to forget what it's like to have a conversation with another person.)

Meanwhile, friends and family in Adelaide lived like Coronavirus hadn't happened. They posted photos of themselves at wineries, at weddings, out to brunch. I scrolled through their photos in my empty house, and then returned to baking a cake for my partner Cameron's big three-oh, which we would celebrate at home. Alone.

Then, we won the fight. We hit zero cases. Cameron and I decided to move back to Adelaide. The dome stayed in place as we called government workers, pleading to be allowed across. Finally, mid-December, we were given a travel pass.

As we drove towards the checkpoint, we fought fears that our border passes would somehow be rescinded. Then we discovered that the border checkpoint had just been dismantled. The police had abandoned the checkpoint. The dome was gone.

On the other side of the border, there hadn't been a case for months. Taking off our masks, our hearts pounded. It felt like a crime. But (masks in hand, just in case) we walked into a busy restaurant, where no one was distancing, and no one was afraid.

A maskless waitress bounded to us with an easy smile, because to her, this wasn't surreal. This wasn't her first time seeing a crowded room in nine months. This wasn't the first time she'd breathed another human's air in hundreds of days without panicking.

And she welcomed us back into normal with the words, 'Merry Christmas. Table for two?'

Sophie

191

BARONESS TANNI GREY-THOMPSON DBE

Welsh politician. TV presenter. Paralympic athlete

Dear Arlo and Kika,

I remember the first time I heard about COVID. I was watching the news with my family and at that point little did we know the devastation it would cause.

Pre-March 2020 it felt like I was always on the move. The phrase 'R number' was not one I ever thought would impact my life, but it all got very real as borders started closing. My husband is a sports coach and he had athletes training in Europe. When they decided to repatriate, I was charged with booking flights and ferries to ensure they could get back. It felt like a race against time.

In a work sense, the Coronavirus legislation brought it home. When over 350 pages of legislation is produced that quickly, you know this is like nothing we have faced before. We had a matter of days to read it and get it through Parliament.

On a personal note, the first few weeks at home were amazing. I was working hard but, without the travelling, I had freedom to be with my family in a way that I have never been able to. Three meals a day

with them felt precious. We have lived through
non-A levels and that felt quite stressful for all of us. I always
admired teachers but I have even more respect for them now. And
then, as so many others found, my free time has been filled with
online meetings.

I love my job in Parliament. There can be long hours and frenetic
speech writing at times, but much of what we do is in a building
that – in some form – has been on that site since 1079. It feels special
every time I walk through the main gates. As a Peer there is a lot you
can do in the chamber, but a cup of tea with colleagues can sometimes
do more. It is the latter that I have missed. Being able to spontaneously
talk to people with different views to my own, to get a sense of which
way a debate is going has been almost impossible online. Though now,
when people now ask, 'How are you?', it feels like they are actually
interested in the answer. I hope this continues.

For athletes this has been an odd year. While training can be
thousands of hours a year, the purpose is to compete. Postponing the
Olympic and Paralympic Games is not something that anyone has
experience of in recent times. Added to this is the uncertainty of what
the selection procedure is going to be, and in what format the games
may go ahead – things beyond an athlete's control. All they can do is
keep training.

The next phase still feels like a big unknown. As we work out how we
return to work, we need to decide whether we want to do it in the
same way. It will take effort to not just drift back to our previous ways
of working. If we can get it right, and can keep hold of lessons the past
year has taught us, I'm excited for what that future looks like.

Tanni Grey-Thompson

SEAN FITZPATRICK
Former New Zealand rugby union
player and All Blacks captain

Dear Arlo and Kika,

Thank you for including me in your project! It was so lovely to hear from you both, what a great idea.

My routine was certainly flipped upside down because of COVID. I am used to being out and about with lots of people, travelling to different cities, and watching lots of different sports. So when I was confined to our house, I busied myself with home improvements. My lawn has never been more meticulously mowed, nor has the house been painted so frequently!

We have two daughters: one is away in the States at university, and the other locked down with my wife and me. I was grateful that I got to spend so much quality time with my family. My wife cooked numerous delicious meals and every weekend we would have a champagne Friday and a special dress-up Saturday night! There was lots of backgammon and bridge going on in our household every evening.

Lacking live sports, I resorted to watching many old games of rugby, which we all enjoyed, but it certainly made me appreciate how lucky we are to be surrounded by live sports all the time.

I stayed on top of my fitness and would jump on the Watt Bike every day to stay focused and in a good mental space.

We had many FaceTimes and Zooms with family and friends, and I did a few podcasts, which was something new for me. Lockdown definitely made me grateful for the small things we take for granted. I feel very humbled by the sacrifices people have made during these exceptional times. I feel very saddened and send my wishes to all those who have been personally affected by the virus.

We are currently now in New Zealand so feel very lucky to be in a mostly COVID-free land. Being able to swim and fish is worth the sacrifice of the late-night Zoom calls up in the UK. We have just finished watching the America's Cup sailing competition, which was such a special moment for our country and a reminder of normal times, with the country being able to come together to celebrate!

We hope that we will be able to do that in the UK very soon.

Sending lots of love from down under,

Sean & Family

195

Sir Mo Farah CBE

Long-distance runner. Four-time
Olympic Champion

Dear Arlo and Kika,

What a pleasure it was to receive your letter. I hope that you are both safe and well, keeping up with your schoolwork and managing not to argue too much! This is a tough time for everyone.

Lockdown has meant that we have all had to make changes to the way we live and sacrifice a lot of the things that we enjoy doing. For me, this has meant a lot more running at home on a treadmill while many races that I had planned – including the 2020 Tokyo Olympic Games – have been postponed or cancelled. However, these competitions mean I am often far away from home at training camps. As I was not able to go, I spent a lot more time at home with my family instead which I very much enjoyed.

I am positive about the future because the world is full of wonderful people just like you. Despite going through a hard and scary time you are thinking of others and what you can do to help them. Rather than tackle this on our own we have to pull together, and everyone has a very important role to play.

History tells us that the world does on occasions encounter times like these, but it also tells us we come through them. You will be able to do all the things you enjoyed doing before, but now they will be even more special because you will realise how precious they are.

Stay patient. Stay kind. Brighter days are ahead.

Sir Mo Farah

PETS AND ANIMALS

DOT McCARTHY
Farmer at Cronkshaw Fold Farm.
Trying to do good stuff for nature

Dear Arlo and Kika,

> 'You know what would be funny? Letting people book our
> goats to join their video calls. Ya know, to spice things up.'

> '. . . WHAT!?'

The global trend to prank workmates, family and friends by randomly
adding a goat to online video calls started life as a joke at the end of a
long, hard, smelly day of shovelling multiple tonnes of poo at our farm,
Cronkshaw Fold, about an hour north of Manchester.

I'd started selling manure when the pandemic hit as I was massively
panicking about running out of money and I was doing anything I could
think of to carry on earning. I'd just taken on my first ever employees
before COVID hit. Their wages were dependent on the income from our
quirky treehouse, yurt and hut hideaways on the farm and hosting
weddings in the barn. All that income had gone. I was desperate to keep
them employed and the business growing. If we stopped earning, I knew
I'd have to dip into savings earmarked for buying solar panels and other
renewable power tech for the farm. I've been saving for YEARS.

15,000+ video calls across more than 50 countries later and GOATS ON ZOOM has not only kept my employees in work and the solar panels savings pot filled, but the goats have had people around the world cracking up with belly laughs, crying into their laptop keyboards with hysterical giggles and trying to keep a straight face in that full meeting where the boss can't figure out which of the two hundred attendees is bleating at them.

Bringing five minutes of silly, confusing, ridiculous joy to tens of thousands of people around the world is something I couldn't even comprehend was possible for a little farm like ours. I am grateful to every single person who booked. We have loved sharing in every grin, bark of surprise and badly concealed snort of laughter that ensued.

Joy is the balm that soothes the frayed edges of the soul.

Dot

CRESSIDA COWELL MBE

Children's author and Waterstones
Children's Laureate

Dear Arlo and Kika,

I'm Cressida Cowell, the writer and illustrator of the
'How to Train Your Dragon' books, and also the current
Waterstones Children's Laureate. Like you, I have missed
friends and family during this difficult year, but lots of
good things have happened too. I work in a little writing
shed at the bottom of my garden, and I have carried
on writing and illustrating there. I love gardening, and
reading and cooking (I'm very greedy), and I've had
more time to do those things. And all of my children
have been at home, which has been lovely. They are a
bit older than you two, so I wasn't having to learn how to
home-school, like a lot of other parents. (I think maybe
Lockdown will have given us a new appreciation for all
the hard work our wonderful teachers do!)

As Children's Laureate, you have a very important role:
to try and help ALL children in the UK discover
the life-changing magic of books. So I thought, what
can I do to help other parents and children who are
having a hard time home-schooling, and dealing with
the pandemic? I find that books are like magical flying
doors, and if you are stuck indoors, they can take you
into other countries, back in time, and put you in someone
else's shoes. I challenged myself to read the whole of
the 'How to Train Your Dragon' books aloud, and I asked
my publisher, Hachette Children's Group, whether as a

special Lockdown treat, they would allow everyone to download it for FREE. And they agreed!

I'm up to book eight. Sometimes things worth doing can take a little time. And you have to push through reading that next chapter, even if you're feeling weary.

Oh, and we got another dog. Our older dog, Pigeon, isn't convinced that this was a good idea. But she's coming round to it . . .

Thank you so much for writing to me. I love your thoughtful letter, and that you are trying to do something helpful for other people. Your response, and the response of so many children and adults like you, are one of the many reasons that I feel positive about the future. Human beings have reacted with extraordinary creativity and organisation and intelligence to the huge challenge they have been faced with. Look how amazing our scientists have been in discovering a vaccine! Look how good most people have been in keeping to the Lockdown rules! If we can do THIS, surely we can tackle the great challenge of climate change with similar determination and success?

I'm going to quote from a great writer, E.B. White, who wrote 'Charlotte's Web': 'Man's curiosity, his relentlessness, his inventiveness, his ingenuity have led him into deep trouble. We can only hope that these same traits will enable him to claw his way out. Hang on to your hat. Hang on to your hope. And wind the clock, for tomorrow is another day.'

Love,
    Cressida Cowell

KATHRYN ENGLAND
Chief Operating Officer, ZSL
London Zoo

Dear Arlo and Kika,

Thank you so much for your delightful letter, and for thinking of us at this strange time.

Life at ZSL London Zoo has certainly been very different over the last year. You asked how we are keeping busy but that is definitely not a problem! Looking after 19,000 animals of all shapes and sizes is a very busy job that needs to be done even if there are no zoo visitors. Our zookeepers have carried on working all the way through three Lockdowns to keep our animals happy and healthy. Some of them even lived in the zoo during Lockdown to be close to their animals! Vets are always on hand as well to keep our animals in the best of health, doing regular check-ups, including on animals like Oni the okapi, who had a baby during Lockdown.

Some of our animals have really missed seeing lots of people, so we've also been paying them special attention. Our pygmy goats are used to being petted and stroked by lots of children, and our zookeepers have been visiting them several times a day just to give them cuddles!

One of our white-cheeked gibbons, Jimmy, loves people-watching and without any visitors he's been calling to joggers in the park outside the zoo trying to get their attention! Our camel Genghis has always been a little nervous about going for walks outside his paddock, so we've been taking him for walks around the quiet zoo and he has gradually got braver and braver. And our alpacas needed a 'Lockdown haircut' earlier this year because their coats had got very long — our zookeepers gave them a lovely trim.

We do feel positive about the future, because we just can't wait to be able to share all these wonderful moments with our visitors again!

Yours sincerely,

Kathryn

Emma Freud OBE
Writer. Broadcaster. Script Editor. Mother. Executive Producer of Comic Relief

Richard Curtis CBE
Writer. Director. Co-Founder of Red Nose Day. Advocate for the UN Sustainable Development Goals

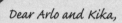

Dear Arlo and Kika,

Thank you for your letter – you're a very impressive pair and this is a really lovely idea.

It feels like the Lockdowns have affected us differently every day. They've made us sad for the pain the pandemic has caused so many millions of people and frightened for the effect it's having on our world.

We're worried about the people who have lost their mums, dads, children, neighbours, their businesses, their income, their security, their health and strength. And also proud for the people who've stepped up to help and been kind and loving to their neighbours and communities – even if that was just clapping. In our own house we're sad for our daughter whose work has been so messed up by it all, but delighted we've got to spend a whole year with her at home. We're concerned that our middle son has spent his first year at university without ever physically going to a lesson, but relieved he's had a great time there anyway. We're worried that our littlest son didn't get to go through that important GCSE learning process, but thrilled he (and we) didn't have to live through those awful exams.

Even our work has been a jumble of emotions! We've produced three big TV shows to raise money for people who are having the toughest time during the pandemic: 'The Big Night In', 'Red Nose Day USA '20', and 'Red Nose Day UK '21' – and we've done them all from our kitchen as our offices have been closed for a year now. So that's been weird. It's been upsetting working on fundraising films about people who were already having so many troubles, and who are now having an even harder battle because of the pandemic. BUT each of the fundraising events has stunned us because of the kindness and care that's been shown to these people as a result: famous people giving their time, artists giving their paintings, businesses giving their money, children giving their imaginations, parents giving their skills, even nurses giving their days off to help people who need support. That's been an incredible thing to see, and if anything can make us optimistic about the future, it's that.

Then two other things have happened which have been amazing – I (Richard) haven't had to go abroad for meetings the entire year, hooray for that . . . and I (Emma) have managed to acquire thirteen new pets. I just snuck them in when nobody was looking. We already had cats, a dog and a tortoise – but we've now added six chickens, a rabbit, five baby ducks (all called Duckface), and a hedgehog called Prickly McPrickface.

Good luck with the book, good luck with your futures, and keep writing letters. You do it really well.

Emma and Richard

VICKI AND CHRIS AGAR

Spring Farm Alpacas is a working alpaca farm set in 110 acres of wildflower meadows and ancient woodland.

Dear Arlo and Kika,

Two of the real joys of Spring Farm are our alpacas (not forgetting the llamas) and our wildlife. Normally, we offer alpaca walking around our beautiful farm in East Sussex to members of the public.

Lockdown had a huge effect on us as a business, as we had to cancel all bookings. The alpacas were particularly unimpressed as they really look forward to their carrot treats at the end of each walk!

Our alpacas' health is paramount to us. Looking after them during Lockdown has given us the time to really help some of the older animals. We have been using acupuncture, physiotherapy and even the healing power of light therapy. Aslan is particularly grateful as he hopes to become a father a few more times in 2021!

We had twenty baby alpacas and one baby llama born in Lockdown. Baby alpacas and llamas are both called 'cria'.

Each year is a different initial for us at Spring Farm for naming the babies. So their names all begin with 'A' except for Señor Snoopy the baby llama – it's a long story!

As we couldn't offer walks to our guests, we had more time to halter train our babies so they can pass their 'walking with guests' exams and join the walking team. This means that when we reopen, there will be new faces to welcome our guests from the halter class of 2020!

We are very excited to be reopening our gates. In 2021, in addition to our walking with alpacas, we will be offering guided meditation with alpacas. Meditating in wildflower meadows surrounded by inquisitive alpacas is going to be a great new experience for us all.

With their big brown eyes and fuzzy smiley faces, spending time around alpacas allows us to take a deep breath. Connecting with nature helps us all to heal, both mentally and physically.

Chris and Vicki Agar

LIFE
ONLINE

RT. HON SIR LINDSAY HOYLE MP

Speaker of the House of Commons
and MP for Chorley

Dear Arlo and Kika,

Thank you for such a lovely, well-written and uplifting letter! As Speaker of the House of Commons and MP for Chorley, you can imagine I get lots of correspondence – and not all of it is cheerful – so your letter made my day.

I love your idea of raising money for children needing extra support after Coronavirus, so I am very happy to contribute a letter to your book.

For me, life in Lockdown has changed considerably. At work, I no longer preside over a packed Chamber of MPs, seeking to 'catch my eye' to speak. Instead, we have screens on either side, with most MPs joining debates from their homes via Zoom. This means question times – like Prime Minister's Questions on

a Wednesday – are particularly quiet.
Debates aren't nearly as noisy, and if
someone goes on longer than need be
in asking a question, I can now mute
them instead of calling out 'Order! Order!'
to get their attention!

Unfortunately, the current restrictions mean my wife, Catherine
– and our pets – can't travel down from our home in Chorley to be
with me in Westminster. While I miss them all, Catherine is rightly
entertained by Boris the parrot, calling out 'Lock the Doors' – which is
a phrase I use in the Chamber when there is a vote – and Patrick, our
ginger-haired Maine Coon cat, who is a brilliant mouser when he is
allowed to patrol the corridors of power.

As for being positive about the future . . . Yes, I am really. The roll-out
of the vaccine is going at an incredible pace – and I am hopeful that
when we have more people vaccinated than not, we can all return to
some sort of normality.

In the meantime, good luck with your fund-raising!

With warmest wishes,

Lindsay

PROFESSOR PATRICIA DALEY

Professor of the Human Geography of Africa, University of Oxford. Vice Principal and Helen Morgan Fellow, Jesus College, Oxford

Dear Arlo and Kika,

Lockdown meant working from home with no physical contact with colleagues or students. The university and college buildings were closed but their activities continued online. As Vice Principal of Jesus College, Oxford, I was involved in making decisions about a range of COVID-19 related measures, from shutting down the college's operations to wellbeing support for students and staff.

In 2020, I was Director of Undergraduate Studies and in charge of moving teaching and examinations online. Work intensified. I listened enviously to stories of people having extra time to bake or develop new hobbies. I had to quickly learn how to use Microsoft Teams, Zoom, and lecture recording software – the mediums for teaching and meetings. 'You're on mute!' became a regular phrase. Cameras invaded the privacy of our colleagues' homes and student bedrooms. Official backgrounds were produced. Since they sometimes distorted the body image, inventive colleagues devised their own – our astrophysicist chose the universe, and our biologist magnified images of small animals

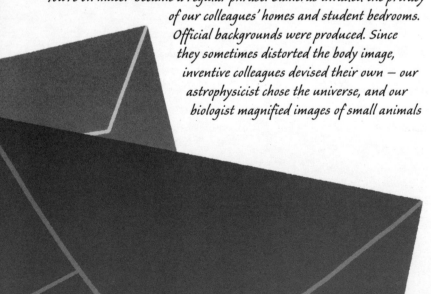

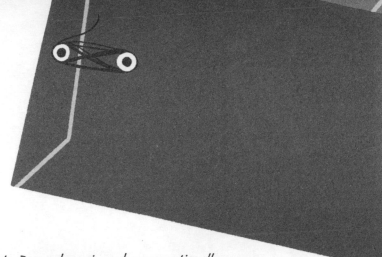

and insects. Research seminars became nationally
and transnationally accessible. Speakers and audiences
across the world (time zones permitting) could participate. I attended
seminars occurring in the USA, the Netherlands, and South Africa.

There were downsides. Students complained of screen fatigue and no
team sports. Repetitive strain injury affected me badly. Fifteen minutes
of intense exercise before work, and a walk after (sometimes with
friends), became mandatory. Through walking the city, I discovered new
green spaces, footpaths, and roads. I became an Urbex (urban explorer)
of Oxford. Lockdown meant spending the longest continuous period in
the city – no travelling to see family in Europe and North America, and
no conferences or fieldwork in East Africa.

Lockdown took my use of digital technologies to a new level. Celebrating
my uncle's diamond wedding anniversary virtually meant seeing
relatives from three continents simultaneously. Zoom Zumba classes,
dance and birthday parties with friends kept me socially connected.
However, I missed face to face contact. I am now convinced that
reading body postures, hand gestures, and eye contact make me
a more effective teacher.

Best wishes,

Patricia Daley

Dr Clare Wenham
Associate Professor of Global
Health Policy, LSE

Dear Arlo and Kika,

I've spent the last decade researching how governments prepare for, and respond to, pandemics. It has been a busy year for me. Each country around the world has done something slightly different in responding to COVID-19, and so the policies developed prior to this pandemic are being put to the test. It has been the hardest year of my professional life, but also the most stimulating.

One of the main areas of my work is understanding how women are affected by epidemics. This has become ever so apparent in the last year. It has been great having parents at home for many kids, but have a think about who is doing your home-schooling, who is playing with you and doing all the additional cooking and cleaning — the data show that this is more likely to be your mother than your father.

This might not seem important, but when we look at it at the country level this means many more women may have lost their jobs to take on this additional stuff at home, and we worry this means women may not find it as easy to return to work when this horrible virus is over.

I am a parent, and as you may know, my daughter interrupted an interview I was giving to BBC, talking about UK government's response to the crisis. I could hear her coming up the stairs to me just as I went live — what was I to do other than carry on?! We've all got so used to merging work and life this year — and now seemingly the whole world knows about my daughter and her love of unicorns. When that video went viral, I had friends and strangers reaching out from across the world saying they'd seen it. I felt a bit sick that it had gone from the spare room to the world, but so many women reached out in solidarity — saying they were going through just the same thing. We've all had to adjust, and the shared experience of parents across the world is something we'll always have to look back on.

Juggling a full-on work schedule with two small children at home is hard. We have been lucky to be able to have childcare support, but I'm so acutely in awe of all the families, whatever these look like, that have been struggling with their work and life in much more difficult circumstances, where parents may be worried about losing their jobs, or with sick family members.

And, let's not forget all the fun we've had. Not being able to go anywhere has meant finding new ways to have fun: building dens, painting with rice, having tea parties, and sleepovers in the living room with family movies. I used to spend a week a month away from my family, having all this additional time with them has really been a blessing, despite the times when I want a break and a glass of wine in peace!

This has been so tough on you kids too — but you'll remember it, and when you look back at it, I hope you recognise how hard your parents must be struggling — and recognise your supermums!

Very best,
        Clare

PAULA TALMAN

Founder of iSpace Wellbeing, the free mental health and wellbeing solution for schools. Director of Compliance, Health and Welfare in Education

Dear Arlo and Kika,

Life in Lockdown has been different for everyone. One way to describe it is that we are all experiencing the same storm but in different boats!

When the first Lockdown began, I didn't really know what to expect and I was overwhelmed by the crash course in online learning that followed. I felt sad and concerned for the many children I cared for in my role as school nurse and health education teacher. How would they manage being torn from their normal lives? How would they cope with online learning and most importantly how would they cope without their friends?

Despite the government's efforts, some children had no access to digital resources and they began to worry about falling behind in their work. One child I spoke to explained how she had to share a mobile phone with four of her siblings! Other children I spoke to couldn't begin to think about their online learning as they were more concerned about where their next meal would come from. Many teachers became superheroes during Lockdown and delivered food parcels to children who

needed them. I thought about what I could do to help too.
I decided I would provide a weekly live 'story time' to help
children across the world look after their mental health and
wellbeing. I also designed a resilience animation to support
teachers and parents in helping themselves and their children
to develop coping tools.

By the end of the first Lockdown, it was evident that children
were exhausted with online learning and they yearned to get
back to school. One child talked of his sadness around the
loss of time, the loss of a birthday celebration and the loss of
family and friendship experiences. Secondary students told
me of their heartache over the stolen opportunity to sit exams.
Although many children had coped with the change and the
challenge many had not and there was a steep rise recorded in
children's mental health issues. There was a crisis in children's
mental health before the pandemic with 1 in 8 children
suffering with a mental health issue but the first Lockdown
saw an increase to 1 in 6.

When Christmas came, my heart sank. It was the first time
in my life that I couldn't be with my family in Ireland. This
disappointment hit my 15-year-old daughter hard too, it was
a break in tradition and a break in the creation of special
family memories. But we got through it, making new traditions
with special parcels sent by post!

Children and young people are among the heroes of this
pandemic. Despite the challenges faced by people so young
they have strived to move forward. We must now encourage
their optimism and hope by preparing and equipping them
mentally, physically, socially and emotionally for the new
journey ahead.

Paula Talman

BILL GATES AND MELINDA FRENCH GATES

Co-Chairs of the Bill and Melinda Gates Foundation

Dear Arlo and Kika,

Greetings from Seattle! We were excited to get your note inviting us to be a part of your project. What a creative way to bring people together at a moment when so many of us are feeling far apart.

For the most part, we've been lucky during the pandemic. Our family is healthy and safe, and we've made the most of the extra time at home — in a typical year, we both do a lot of travelling for work. Instead, we've seen more of each other and our youngest daughter, Phoebe. (Our two older kids, Jenn and Rory, don't live at home anymore. Jenn is in medical school, and Rory is in college.)

If you're doing remote learning, then our days probably look pretty similar: lots and lots of time in front of the computer. We started our careers in the technology industry, so we're used to staring at computer screens — but it's been a new experience to spend entire days in back-to-back video calls. We try to sneak in little breaks when we can. One of us (Melinda) takes a lot of walks and fits in a lot of Netflix. The other (Bill) is playing even more online bridge than ever.

That said, it's been a really busy year for us at work. Twenty-one years ago, we started a foundation dedicated to helping people everywhere have the chance to live a healthy, productive life. We've been focused on a number of issues that have become even more important during the pandemic — like developing new vaccines and getting them to people in low-income countries, and supporting students who may be falling behind at school. We're proud of the way our colleagues at the foundation and its partners have stepped up to respond to the pandemic, and we're going to keep working hard to help get vaccines, medicine, and economic relief to the people who are hurting the most.

You asked in your letter if we're optimistic about the future. Our answer is yes! There's no question it's been a challenging year and a lot of people have suffered — so it's easy to understand why you're feeling uncertain about what's ahead. But we think there are a lot of reasons to be hopeful. One big one is that, as we write this, hundreds of millions of vaccine doses have already been distributed and more people are getting one every day. That's a major step towards putting the pandemic behind us and returning to some sort of normalcy.

We're also optimistic because we've seen so many people coming together to make sure that as the world recovers, no one is left behind. What you're doing to raise money for vulnerable children is a perfect example! We're inspired by your project, and we hope it is just the start of a lifelong habit of giving back.

There are a lot of lessons that the world has learnt over the past year. One of the most important ones is that we're all connected, and we need to take care of each other. If more people carry that lesson forward with them after the pandemic is over, we believe the world will be a better place — and that the future you'll grow up in will be full of new possibilities.

Take care,

Bill and Melinda

FERGUS LLEWELLYN
Headmaster, Cumnor House Sussex

Dear Arlo and Kika,

In this world of email and text messaging, it is a delight to receive a letter through the post, especially one as thoughtful and as well-written as yours.

You pose some interesting questions, which have caused me to reflect on our recent lives. Like many people, we experienced frustrations, uncertainty, disappointment, and irritation in having our normal freedoms, patterns of life, and opportunities to vary our days taken away from us. For our family, who are new to the area, we are certainly mourning the fact that we cannot connect properly with neighbours, forge new friendships and build a new community.

This leads me to perhaps the biggest challenge I am facing personally, as Headmaster of a new school, namely that I find it very hard to lead in an environment where connecting with people is such a challenge. Leadership relies on the importance of building relationships, sensing how people are doing, picking up clues in body language or conversation, and bringing the right amount of support or challenge to help them get better. I really miss not bumping into children around school, chatting to them, watching them interact. I have popped into some online lessons, but with so many cameras off, it is hard to gauge everyone's mood.

This remains a big challenge for me, and one that I am trying all the time to adapt to and be creative about. I am a great believer that in life, we never stop learning. It has never been more important for us to reflect on what we are doing, and ask ourselves searching questions, challenging ourselves to not settle for the status quo, but look to get better every day.

This sentiment is also the reason why I remain very optimistic about the future. Humans have a fantastic capacity to use their collaborative and creative ingenuity and resourcefulness to rise and conquer whatever challenges are thrown their way. Your letter, for example, is a wonderful demonstration of two young people wanting to rise above the challenges of their lives, look beyond their immediate horizons, and learn from other people. With such a spirit, there is always hope and cause for optimism.

I hope that, in amongst the gloom of Lockdown, you can lift your heads up, look positively at the future, and walk with confidence and hope.

Yours,

Fergus

Arlo and Kika
A Farm in Sussex
England

223

PAUL MORRISON
Youth mentor. Founder of Idare2inspire.
STEM Ambassador. Zoomie

Dear Arlo and Kika,

The pandemic has changed our lives in so many ways and for a lot of people it has been one of the most challenging times ever. That also includes me!

When the pandemic started I couldn't believe what was happening around me. Sadly, the virus wreaked havoc throughout my community resulting in too many of my friends and family members losing their precious lives. It was like watching a scary movie that made me feel incredibly empty and often scared.

But I like helping others and was determined to turn my own sadness into caring for those who were feeling lost and alone.

I decided to leave my job so I could support my community in the best way possible. I love to cook, so I prepared delicious meals for people who were either homeless or socially isolated. I cooked some of my favourite dishes including roast chicken and potatoes, rice, pasta bake and lots of fresh vegetables. It made me feel incredibly proud to see that my cooking was able to make people smile again, at least for a short time.

I also got an exciting new job at Zoom, where I help schools to use video communications technology, so that teachers and students can participate in classes no matter if they are in the school or at home. Maybe you have taken part in one of those virtual classrooms yourself? I know it is not the same as seeing your friends and classmates in person but I hope it helped you to keep in touch during these months of extraordinary circumstances.

At Zoom we will always be extremely proud to have been able to help you and everyone else stay connected with friends and family during the pandemic. One thing to recognise is that when we were focused on helping people get connected, all my colleagues were also going through the same emotions as everyone else – fear, uncertainty, worry. But getting through this difficult time together has been an extremely humbling learning experience and has given everyone at Zoom a newfound appreciation of what it means to be a video communications technology provider in times of need.

I don't know what the future will hold but just remember: 'Believe in yourself and all that you are. Know that there is something inside of you that is greater than any obstacle.' (Christian D. Larson).

Best wishes,

Paul Morrison

HEALTH AND
WELLBEING

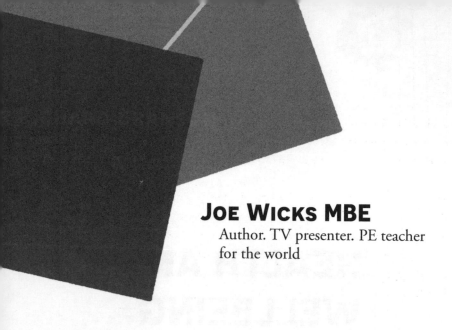

JOE WICKS MBE
Author. TV presenter. PE teacher for the world

Dear Lockdown,

I want to start by saying thank you. Why? I know you came at a terrible time and you were so hard on many people, but I want to say thanks for the people I've seen rise to your challenge and become stronger. Because of you, 'PE with Joe' was born, and at 9am Monday to Friday all through Lockdown, millions of people from around the world came together in that very moment. We danced, we star jumped, we bunny hopped and burpeed all around the room. We smiled, we laughed, we forgot about everything negative and for a moment felt truly present and happy. We had so much fun with fancy dress Fridays, playing spot the difference and learning exciting new things with the morning quizzes.

In total we came together and completed 115 workouts and 100 million people took part!

We had children in India, grandparents in Australia, schools in Ireland and families in Brazil all taking part. We built a global community and I'm so proud to say that, together, we raised over £610k for NHS charities and BBC Children in Need — at a time when they couldn't have needed it more.

Those of us who took part came out fitter, stronger, and healthier. We kept turning up no matter how we were feeling. We always came out with a smile and a positive and optimistic mindset. We learnt the true value of exercising, for not just our physical health but our mental health too, both of which the last year really put to the test.

My one hope is this: that when the community of people who tuned in at 9am look back at Lockdown they have fond memories of 'PE with Joe' as a bright point in a difficult time. I wish with all my heart that it has inspired a generation of young children to love exercise and live a healthy and happy life.

Love, Joe Wicks, PE teacher for the world!

DR ALEX GEORGE

Doctor. Author. Youth Mental
Health Ambassador

Dear Arlo and Kika,

Thank you SO much for your letter. I hope you are both doing OK. I am sorry you haven't seen your friends in a while, but I hope you have been able to catch up with them back at school. I also haven't seen my friends or family for a long time as I live alone in London. I have been very lucky though, because I also have a family where I work.

I am a doctor working in a London hospital. It has been a really busy year looking after patients with COVID-19. Everyone in the NHS has worked so hard and we have been one big family, caring for each other as well as our patients. I was very grateful for everyone who went outside to clap for us each Thursday – it really helped us feel happy and positive. Although this year has been hard on all of us I think it has taught us how important it is to help each other when we can. It helps us all to be kind.

In my role as Youth Mental Health Ambassador, I'm trying to make mental health a positive issue. I want to make sure young people think about their mental health in the same way they think about physical health. So many young people have suffered in the past year and going back to school doesn't erase that. I'm pushing for more trained mental health professionals to be present in schools, and for easier access to

counsellors. In the meantime, I would encourage every child —
and adults too — to talk about anything they're anxious about,
whether with friends, family, or teachers. Don't ever hesitate
to ask for help.

Looking forward to the future, I feel very positive, there is a
light at the end of the tunnel for us all. The vaccine is helping
to protect us from COVID-19 and we will be able to enjoy
life again. I also feel that the last year has taught us all to
treasure health and happiness. I hope that we will continue to
enjoy being outside in the fresh air,
exercising and being thankful for the
little things in life. I am so excited
to see my friends and family
again and give them all a big hug.

Thank you so much for your
letter, I hope you will get to
play with your friends soon.

Best wishes,

Dr Alex

LAURA ELLIOTT
Disability writer. Journalist.
Campaigner

Dear Arlo and Kika,

When you hear the word 'Lockdown' it's easy to think of something bad, like the world is getting smaller and things are being taken away. It sounds like a key being turned in a lock and shutting everyone inside.

But sometimes, when you turn a key, it opens a door instead of closing it, and that's what it was like for me.

When the first Lockdown started, I was already very sick with an illness called M.E., which can make people too unwell to leave their beds. I hadn't been able to leave my house much for four very long years, and I had sometimes been quite lonely. It's difficult to do things like work, and learn, and watch concerts and theatre when you can't go outside.

But when everyone else had to stay home as well, something amazing happened. A key turned in a lock, and my world opened up again.

Theatres started to stream shows online. Learning was done over Zoom. Jobs wanted people to work from home, and friends hosted video quizzes every weekend.

Sometimes, it makes me sad to realise that it was always so easy to do. If more people had cared a long time ago, then maybe I'd always have been able to work, and learn, and enjoy more things from inside. There are lots of people in the world like me who have lived in Lockdown for years.

Now that we're coming to the end for you, I hope that when everyone goes back to normal, some of the new things remain.

I hope theatres will still let me watch from home. I hope jobs will still let me work from my bed, and I hope friends will still want to do quizzes on Zoom on the nights they don't go outside.

Even though it was hard and the world has seemed quite scary, for some of us this Lockdown, the key turned in the lock the right way, and we got to see more of the good things again.

Laura

DAVINA McCALL
TV presenter and fitness advocate

Dear Arlo and Kika,

Well, this is brilliant! I haven't written a proper letter, on writing paper in . . . it must be DECADES! I have bought writing paper especially for this! I might actually go letter writing mad! It's such a lovely thing to do. And they are so nice to receive. It's been a crazy year! A WHOLE YEAR?

I have three kids, Chester, 14; Tilly, 17 and Holly, 19. And I suppose my biggest worry in Lockdown has been their mental health. They started off really missing their friends, but now they are a bit nervous about going back to 'normal'.

Have you been able to exercise? I've tried to stay super active. I have a dog called Bo, and Bo has always cheered me up when I've been sad! She's always happy to see me, she's very cuddly and even when I've just lost the motivation to move, she still needs walking, so it gets me out in nature and gets me some fresh air in my lungs. I've always said, 'I've never regretted a workout,' but I can honestly say I've never regretted a walk either. Time to breathe, get off my phone, commune with my dog and decompress. And then, best of all, a half hour workout after, to make me feel strong and full of life!

Thank you so much for inspiring me to write! I have enjoyed it so much.

Lot of love and hugs, Davina

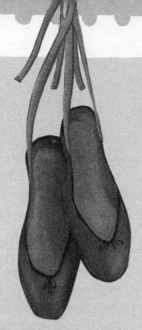

Tamara Rojo CBE

English National Ballet's Artistic
Director and a lead principal dancer

Dear Arlo and Kika,

Thank you for your interest in how the
pandemic has affected English National Ballet.

When we first went into Lockdown we were only one week away from
the world premiere of a new ballet by the choreographer Akram Khan.
We had been rehearsing for many weeks, the orchestra had been
working on the score, and the sets and costumes were finished. All the
tickets had been sold months before. The audience was really looking
forward to this new piece, so it was hard to have to cancel the shows.

I know how important training is for dancers' mental and physical
health, and that dancers all over the world would no longer have
access to studios and classes. So, from the very first day of Lockdown
I started to teach class every morning from my kitchen. I was very
surprised that at the end of the ten weeks, during which I shared
these lessons for free, we had four million views — so many people had
joined me in the everyday ceremony of ballet class! It was not easy to
keep motivated and teach every morning, but the messages arriving
from around the world kept me going.

Finally, in August we were able to return to the studios and
we started straight away on creating new works, following the

restrictions on number of dancers and lack of touch. We hoped to present these works live on stage in the autumn, but once again this was not possible due to further Lockdown measures.

The same happened again when, the day before opening night, we had to cancel our Christmas run of 'The Nutcracker'. It was heart-breaking to tell all the artists, costume makers, musicians, and technical staff that we couldn't go ahead after all the work and dedication they had put into making it happen. ENB had been performing Nutcracker every year since our birth 70 years ago, so we decided to film it and share it for free with our audiences as a thank you, and to try to lift their spirits during these difficult times.

Personally, I was set to make my first choreography last year: 'Raymonda', inspired by the figure of Florence Nightingale. I was so excited, as I have been researching and preparing for five years, and because 2020 was the 200th anniversary of her birth, there were many celebrations throughout the year in her honour. It seems almost ironic that 2020 was going to become a year in which her work and the dedication of nurses all over the world would be so important. Although I will now have to wait until 2022 for this to premiere, I do feel that at this time it will be an even more poignant homage to Florence and the nursing profession.

Your book will be a wonderful memory for generations to come of this challenging year in human history. Thank you for inviting me to be part of it.

Tamara Rojo

COLONEL DAME KELLY HOLMES DBE

Double Olympic gold medalist. Author. Entrepreneur. Fitness and mental health champion

Dear Arlo and Kika,

I'm so pleased to be able to write this letter to say that, even though 2020 was a massive disruption for all of us, we got through it.

That said, though we've lived through it together, we've each coped with it differently. I'm very lucky to have a garden but I know so many other people haven't had that space, or have been isolated, or have had worries around financial and work issues.

I got Covid and it was a scary time. I suffered with the after-effects for about eight to ten weeks. During that time I'd lost my sense of smell and taste. It didn't matter if I'd had chilli, toothpaste, peanut butter, marmite, sweets or a gin and tonic. Whatever I had it all tasted the same and that was really bizarre! Most of all it really zapped my energy which then made me feel low. I was so pleased that I was able to force my mind into activity and to keep my body moving. It really helped.

During Lockdown One I started a fitness brand called 'Military in Motion' to try and inspire people to keep an active life for their wellbeing, mental health as well as physical health. This has grown into a great community of people who have motivated, inspired and supported each other to be the best version of themselves. This makes me feel really proud.

We should remember that in society you are a human being first and foremost, before being an employee or somebody that has to do something for other people.

I would say to everybody: live with hope, flick the switch, put the most positive attitude you can on to 2021. We will get through this and I wish everybody a successful year and beyond.

Best wishes,
  Colonel Dame Kelly Holmes (MBE mil)

ADAPTATION

ANTONY CAUVIN

Plasterer and inventor of the 'Cuddle Curtain'

Dear Arlo and Kika,

When Boris Johnson made the hard decision to put us into Lockdown on 23rd March 2020, my wife and I were meant to be out celebrating our second wedding anniversary, but instead we were at home watching the news like everyone else! My wife was already preparing to work from home, but things were a little more uncertain for me. I am a plasterer and going into the homes of others is how I make my living. To keep others safe, I had to sacrifice my work.

I am very fortunate that all my family live nearby and we are very close, especially my grandparents, so being able to see them (even from a distance) is what kept me motivated. My wife and I would visit my grandparents from the garden and talk to them in their conservatory. But as the months passed it got harder to see my Grannan struggling not being able to share a hug.

So . . . I set to work! I wanted to create a method to hug my Grannan whilst keeping her safe. I spent some time

242

creating a frame using bits of wood and an old curtain pole across the top. I ordered a clear shower curtain, some gauntlets and protective sleeves. Through trial and error, and some rather hilarious negotiations with my wife, I was able to position the arm holes in just the right places. A shower curtain, suspended from a curtain pole, with four arm holes cut out and replaced with protective sleeves! Ta-da! The Cuddle Curtain was created! I was confident in my design, so I didn't hang about . . .

I turned up in my grandparents garden that afternoon and announced I WAS going to hug my Grannan. Armed with anti-bac spray and enough gauntlets to go around, it enabled me and some family members to be able to safely share an incredible hug. Even more incredibly, the video we posted of our hug was viewed millions of times and was picked up in the news. I was so happy to hear that it had sparked hope and joy in the hearts of so many others.

Life is getting back to normal now and I'm excited for the future. If the past year has taught me anything, it's that adversity and struggle can bring people together. I certainly appreciate the simpler things in life more now. Stay grateful that you had each other through these strange times and one day you will look back and realise how much you learnt.

Stay safe,

Antony Cauvin

NINA RAINGOLD

Portrait photographer

Dear Arlo and Kika,

It's been a strange year. In the new 'normal' we have spent more time in our homes than ever before. Home is the beating heart of family life but it has taken on many new meanings recently. It has been a refuge, a place to keep safe from the outside world, to protect ourselves and others from getting sick. It has also been a place where we may have felt trapped, from where we have dreamt of the outside world and the everyday things we had taken for granted like playgrounds, bus rides, family get-togethers and holidays. Some of our homes have transformed into schools and offices, as well as the places where we normally eat, sleep and spend time together.

As a family photographer, I'm lucky enough to get invited into people's homes and to temporarily be part of their family lives, with all its chaos, love, drama and excitement. This is a huge privilege and one that, perhaps, I had previously taken for granted. This year, restrictions have meant that it has not been possible for me to work as I usually would.

However, I have been able to embark on a special project photographing mothers who have given birth during the pandemic and recording their stories. I have had the honour of sharing the familial spaces of these women and their new babies (from a safe social distance!), some of whom have never met their grandparents and never been held by anyone other than their parents. For these babies, the four walls of their home are all they have ever known. They have so much to learn about what the world can be, about social interactions and human contact. The home has been a sanctuary for their mothers, but so much time spent inside, rather than out in the world meeting people and getting the support and comfort that new mothers rely on, has been isolating and a big challenge.

I hope that as time progresses, we will slowly get back to the old 'normal', where we can once again share our homes with others and put ourselves back out into the world.

Best wishes,

Nina Raingold

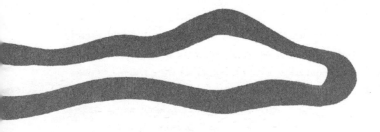

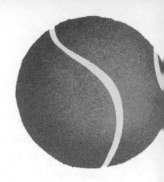

SANDI PROCTER
Kids tennis specialist and volunteer.
Deputy President of the LTA (Lawn
Tennis Association)

Dear Arlo and Kika,

In my role as Deputy President of the LTA (Lawn Tennis Association), I
would normally be busy with meetings and visits to clubs and tournaments.
Lockdown changed all that but I did take enormous delight in seeing how
the tennis community faced up to the challenge.

Players of all ages were brilliant at recreating tennis at home. LTA social
media said 'Play Your Way' and everyone did. People played in the garden
over a rope or the washing line, indoors over the couch, with household
implements like frying pans and hitting into a wheelie bin. Exploits were
shared online to inspire and entertain others. Andy Murray challenged fans
to hit a 100-volley rally and post a video — which thousands did. Another
challenge featured trick shots with a racket and toilet roll — putting the
videos together so it looked like one long loo-roll rally (don't mention the
UK loo roll shortage!). Lots of money was raised for charity.

Some families chalked out lines in their garden and pretended to
be at Wimbledon. And whilst we were sad when the actual
Championships were cancelled, we were treated to some
new events called 'Battle of the Brits', TV re-runs of
classic matches and stories of famous tennis players.
I particularly liked the one about Althea Gibson who

was the first black player to win a Grand Slam. We watched at home with our strawberries and cream, while the actual strawberries grown for the tournament were donated by the Championships to local food banks. NHS workers were treated to a day playing on the hallowed grass courts at Wimbledon, whilst around the country tennis clubs offered free lessons to NHS workers and indoor centres opened up as vaccination centres.

Staying connected has been important for all of us, and, within the tennis community, we did a good job. We'll look back at this time as a period of sadness and disappointment, but also one of great resilience, adaptation and innovation. We are mindful of those amongst us, and in the wider world, who have suffered loss and faced difficulties. We'll work hard to come back stronger, to bring people back together and use the new skills we've learnt.

Some time ago, I had the idea of the red, orange, and green stages of kids' tennis balls. Now, when anyone tries tennis for the first time, they find it much easier using the softer balls. Following Lockdown there's been a surge of new players to the courts and I hope to see lots of red tennis balls out there. Now, we're all looking forward to a summer of tennis and the return of Wimbledon — the grass courts are looking immaculate. They did have a year off after all.

Sandi Procter

SIR RICHARD BRANSON

Entrepreneur. Investor. Author.
Founder of The Virgin Group

Dear Arlo and Kika,

Thank you for asking me to write a letter about how my Lockdown has been and whether I'm optimistic about the future.

As a proud grand-dude to five wonderful, inquisitive grandchildren, it is so pleasing to see other children keeping their eyes and ears open to the world, asking questions and coming up with great ideas like this book. That's certainly one thing that gives me a lot of hope for the years ahead.

I have been in business for fifty years and 2020 was the most challenging yet: our planes were grounded, our hotels and health clubs closed, and our cruise ships confined to port. At the heart of it, a business is just a group of people and it really broke my heart seeing how the pandemic affected our people around the world.

However, my mum, who sadly passed away from COVID, taught me to always bounce back. I've had her words in my head as I spent my lockdown working closely with all our teams around the world to try and make sure that <u>all</u> of our businesses and employees make it through the pandemic. I have also made sure to keep fit and healthy and that has helped me stay in a positive frame of mind.

I am an optimist for the future. In our greatest challenges we often discover the greatest opportunities for positive change. The pandemic has taught us that with collaboration and unity, humanity can solve giant problems.

This is how we move forward – together.

Best,

Richard Branson

ZOË BURKE
Social Media Editor, *Hitched*

Dear Arlo and Kika,

My name is Zoë, and I'm a wedding journalist. Weddings are the most special things: joyous, occasions built on celebrating love, as well as the lifeblood of many small businesses all over the country.

Weddings were hit hard by the pandemic — as the first Lockdown began, so many couples had their big days, which they'd saved up for and eagerly counted down to, cancelled with no notice. This broke hearts everywhere — for those couples, but also for all the businesses who couldn't get to work doing what they love. Our survey showed that a staggering 71% of weddings in 2020 couldn't go ahead as planned.

I returned to work in June 2020, after having a baby, Matilda. I came into a workplace where instead of writing up wedding stories and sharing advice, we looked at how to support businesses with no income, and to encourage couples to keep the faith in a hard and trying time.

I've been so inspired by this incredible industry — I've worked with wonderful people across the UK Weddings Taskforce,

individuals who gave so much time for free
to lobby for support and fair treatment for
weddings. You might have seen them on the news!

I've also spoken to so many couples — couples who turned their
150-strong weddings into garden gatherings of immediate
family, and pulled together flawless, unforgettable days built
on pure love, with just weeks of notice.

One particular couple stands out — Jessica and Jonathan
Cope. They had to rearrange their wedding three times and
desperately lobbied for clear guidance and support. They
planned a wedding for six, for fifteen, for thirty, for fifty
and for 180 — a guestlist for all scenarios. They had three
separate wedding dates and two possible venues, due to
confusing and conflicting guidance. They finally married on the
first day ceremonies could resume again — a party of six, not
at the venue they initially planned and without many of the
suppliers they initially booked. But they did it, and they're
married!

Their story isn't unique — this has been a strange and
difficult time for weddings. But we're coming back now, we're
ready to celebrate life and love together again.

Next time you go to a wedding, take it all in. Think about
how many people work together to make such a beautiful
event happen. Appreciate being surrounded by happy people
celebrating love — it's not ever something to be taken for
granted, especially after the year we've all had.

Yours,

Zoë Burke

SCOTT EVANS (MR EVANS)
Reader. Teacher. 'The Reader Teacher'

Dear Arlo and Kika,

Thank you very much for your letter.

My name is Scott Evans but most people call me 'Mr Evans' as I'm a primary school teacher, or 'The Reader Teacher' because I love reading children's books. I teach a mixed Year 5 and Year 6 class.

Usually, I would build up a really good relationship with my classes in person over the year by doing lots of activities with them like residential trips and transition days to their new secondary schools. However, this has been very different recently as my classes of children have only had me as their in-person teacher for approximately half a school year because of Lockdown. It was also a bit of a shock when the first Lockdown was announced because our school inspection was cancelled on the day it was supposed to take place!

Turning the lights off and closing the door to my classroom, saying goodbye to the children, to the parents and to the rest of the school on Friday, 20th March 2020 was an incredibly surreal experience to say the least. This was all happening too soon. Four months too soon. We expect to bid farewell to each other at the end of July, not March, and we really didn't know when we would see everyone all together in real life again.

We couldn't predict what home learning would be like. It was quite strange to begin with. Live lessons on Zoom, online marking and workouts with Joe Wicks became the normal routine for the day (even for some of us teachers!). But what I liked seeing the most from my classes was how families came together in different ways, whether sharing stories, getting outdoors for activities, or just spending more time together.

Being back in school recently has shown us all how important it is to reconnect with the people around you, including your friends and your teachers. During these unprecedented times, I hope that we have found the time to reconsider and realise what is important to us and that, going forward, we make sure to be kind to everyone and recognise what we can do to help each other and those around us to be happy.

I hope you are keeping well!

Mr Evans

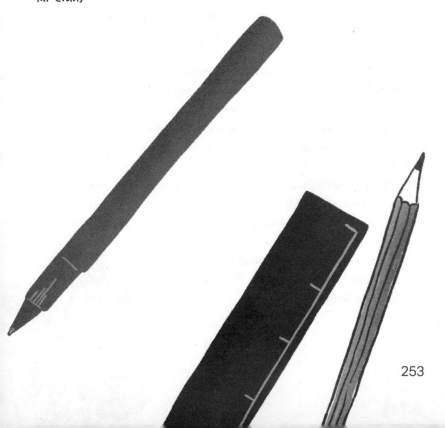

PHILIPPA CRADDOCK

Founder and Creative Director of
Philippa Craddock Design Studio
and Flower School

Dear Arlo and Kika,

Thank you for your lovely letter. I really enjoyed reading it and I think it is wonderful that you are connecting with so many different people when we have all been feeling disconnected from one another. Just like you. I have missed my friends enormously. As a family though, we have been making the very best of the time we have all had together, and I have been very grateful for that.

I am a florist and I create large designs with fresh flowers for clients all over the world. When Lockdown first happened, we were all told we could no longer meet up in large gatherings, so creating flower designs for weddings and events came to a stop. Many florists adapted, creating doorstep deliveries and selling their flowers online.

I love designing with flowers and being creative; whilst in Lockdown in Dorset, where I live, I discovered local flower growers had excess flowers as they were no longer supplying to local restaurants, shops and events, and I wondered if we could create a network between growers, florists and people confined to their homes, to be creative with flowers.
So I did three things:

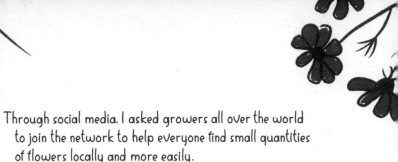

- Through social media, I asked growers all over the world to join the network to help everyone find small quantities of flowers locally and more easily.

- I filmed how-to guides, to show people how to create with flowers.

- And I connected with many different people through a love of flowers and I heard their stories.

Flowers play such an important part in making me happy, connecting and designing directly with nature, and I know they do the same for many people. I believe Lockdown was an unexpected opportunity for all of us to slow down a little and spend time in one place. In Dorset we are very lucky to have access to local woodlands and the sea.

You asked if I feel positive about the future. I believe the future is up to us: we have a choice and it's always better to choose to be positive.

It's also important to dream big! Someone once said to me, 'If you know how you are going to achieve your goals, your goals are not big enough'. This always makes me smile and it reminds me to choose positivity and to dream big! I think you are already achieving exactly that with your amazing goal of publishing 'Letters From Lockdown'. I love your big dream. I am certain you will succeed, and in doing so, you will make many, many people happy.

WELL DONE!

With huge love,

Philippa x

REFLECTION

ALICE M. GREENWALD
President and CEO National
September 11 Memorial & Museum

Dear Arlo and Kika,

Your project to collect these stories of hardship and hope during Lockdown is deeply meaningful, as is your intention to raise funds for children who have suffered due to the COVID-19 pandemic.

On a personal level, I have felt fortunate. The worst part of Lockdown for me was being unable to hold my newest grandchild until quite recently. Judah was born in early August, and I finally held him in my arms for the first time in February!

What I most want to share with you is how COVID affected my professional life. I run the 9/11 Memorial & Museum in Manhattan. Like so many cultural institutions, the Memorial & Museum was forced to close temporarily last March due to the crisis. This had some severe consequences. Our primary source of income had always come from Museum attendance — and with six months of closure, we were faced with (and continue to face) unprecedented financial challenges.

Still, we have remained committed to our mission, thanks to the generosity and unwavering support of our members and donors, the exceptional leadership of our Chairman and Board of Trustees, and a professional staff whose dedication and creativity are unequalled. The pandemic taught me about human beings' capacity for adaptation. As my staff navigated uncharted waters, we all learnt how to work remotely, and we successfully converted much of our on-site programming to online formats.

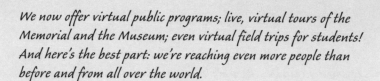

We now offer virtual public programs; live, virtual tours of the Memorial and the Museum; even virtual field trips for students! And here's the best part: we're reaching even more people than before and from all over the world.

For me, the most profound lesson of this difficult time is something we teach at the Museum: that, in the face of adversity and unfathomable loss of life, our capacity for hope and resilience will see us through. As we confronted the shock and grief of the present moment and witnessed the outpouring of gratitude and encouragement for those on the front lines of response to COVID, we saw something familiar from 9/11 history. Then, as now, so many people came out to cheer on those who — selflessly and courageously — rushed to help.

Though the Memorial & Museum attests to one of the most awful events imaginable, it is nevertheless seen worldwide as a symbol of healing, renewal, and hope in the aftermath of tragedy. We of course document the story of a terrorist attack, but what we collect, preserve, and share are stories of leadership, courage, service, and sacrifice. These stories resonate deeply at this moment, as we are confronting the worst global health crisis in over a century. I believe they will continue to be instructive and inspirational in the face of challenges we cannot yet imagine. If 9/11 teaches us anything, it is that we can prevail, we can rebuild, and we will keep moving forward together, all the while remembering, honouring, and preserving history.

So, my COVID Lockdown story is really one about people caring for others, responding and adapting, and remembering that, in the worst situations, hope is still possible. And, because of that, I do feel positive about the future.

I look forward to meeting you in person one day. Until then, stay safe and well and curious and, most of all, hopeful!

Alice M. Greenwald

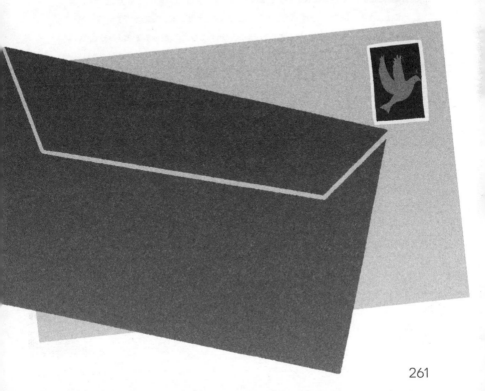

TOBY REGBO
Actor

Dear Arlo and Kika,

I spent a lot of last year's Lockdown by myself in
my flat, watching the news unfold on my computer
screen and staying sane by taking art classes
online. It's difficult to remember the specifics
because those weeks and months have blended
together like pancake batter. All the usual
markers of date and time, the birthdays, the
Sunday roasts, were all cancelled or, at best,
relegated to Zoom.

It certainly was a lesson in how to be alone
without being lonely. I missed being with my
family and friends. I missed things I never
thought I would, like crowded rooms and noisy
restaurants.

Though Lockdown turned life upside down and
was extremely hard on the film industry, and the
arts as whole, I am grateful for certain things I
learnt during that time. Amidst the solitude, the

24-hour news cycle, all the uncertainty, I think the Lockdown created a space for reflection. It temporarily hit pause on the rat race. Always somewhere to be, someone to see, a meeting to sprint to. In pre-Lockdown times if I stayed at home I felt guilty. But for a moment that pressure was gone. Of course, there was fear: about work (or the lack of it) and what the future held, but for a brief while last year there was this quiet reflective space. Even the sky was free of aeroplanes.

Over the summer I got to know my neighbours through our open windows. We rallied together from a distance. 'Can I get you anything?' became our catchphrase. There was a feeling that we were all in this together, against our collective invisible foe. Not just our street but the whole city. The country. The world. It felt powerful to be part of this vast shared human experience.

Above all, the Lockdown left me with a deep sense of gratitude. My family is safe and healthy. Every day I am bowled over by the stories of incredible heroism, of doctors, nurses, key workers, how quickly a small business can start producing masks or delivering meals to those in need.

I feel grateful for the normal, the humdrum, the everyday. It's only when the normal is taken away you realise just how special it really is.

Toby

ALI MERCER
Women's fiction author

Dear Arlo and Kika,

Already the early days of Lockdown seem a long way back: the loo roll shortage, the clear blue skies, the freshly felt-tipped rainbows in people's windows, the banana bread . . .

One of my abiding memories of the past year will be the sight of my thirteen-year-old son Tom disappearing ahead of me down towpaths and country lanes. He is autistic and has a learning disability, and he did not like home school at all. However, he did like discovering new walks in and around our hometown of Abingdon in Oxfordshire: Swift Ditch, Larkhill Stream and Peep-O-Day Lane, to name just a few. We are lucky to have so much calming green space nearby.

Something else I will always remember is the sound of my seventeen-year-old daughter Izzy upstairs in her bedroom, playing her guitar. She found that music, reading, writing and films were ways to go to other places when we weren't able to in real life. Her prom dress is still hanging up in her bedroom unworn – we never got as far as finding shoes to match. Maybe one day . . .

Day-to-day life in Lockdown has shrunk to our little bubble, but going to the doctor to have my first dose of the vaccine gave me a glimpse of the huge scale of the effort we are all part of to get through this. We didn't need to queue to get our jabs, but everybody formed an orderly socially-distanced line anyway! I came away feeling very grateful.

The next day I noticed something I hadn't even realised I had missed. It was lunchtime at the primary school round the corner, the one my two used to go to, and I heard the sound of children playing. That's one of the most hopeful sounds there is.

There is so much to look forward to!

Love to you and your family from everyone here,

Ali Mercer

MARO ITOJE

Professional rugby
player for England
and Saracens

Dear Arlo and Kika,

Thank you for writing to me! I really enjoyed reading about what you have both been up to during the various Lockdowns. Thank you also for all of your support, especially you, Arlo.

Lockdown was a period of great reflection for me. Often in life you feel as if you do not have time to stop and take stock and appreciate everything you have, as the focus is always on what is happening next and what the next goal is — this is definitely the case in professional sport. This means you don't always fully appreciate things when they happen. Lockdown gave me the time and space to reflect and, in periods when there was a lot of negativity going on in the world, it gave me time to be grateful for all the amazing people in my life. I have a greater appreciation for my loved ones, family and friends as a result. It also made me extremely grateful to be able to play the game I love and appreciate how lucky I am. Going forward I am definitely going to try to be more present and appreciate events more in the moment.

I tried to use Lockdown to rest and recover from what has been an extremely busy year for me, but I also tried to use it to make me a more rounded person. I started studying for my masters, reading lots of books and listening to podcasts, as well as training really hard to make sure I was in the best possible shape for when rugby restarted again. But most importantly I tried to maintain and build stronger connections to the people that matter most.

Best wishes,
　　Maro

Dame Helen Mirren DBE
Actress

Dear Arlo and Kika,

Thank you for your letter.

New words: Lockdown, Quarantine.

New normals: masks, hand sanitizer, pressing buttons with your elbow, standing six feet away from someone in a queue, going to school on a computer — just one year ago how strange all of that would have sounded.

Before 'Lockdowns' only happened in prisons and 'Quarantine' happened to dogs coming from abroad.

Of course, it was, and still is, a very different experience for each of the nearly 8 billion people on this planet who have been affected, but we do all have that one thing in common; we experienced it.

For me it was a time to experience the simple pleasure of having dinner with my husband every night, something that was not possible before because I was so often away working.

It was a time to feed the birds and the chipmunks, and inadvertently the odd bear! (I'm currently stuck in America) I've been endlessly entertained by them.

It was a time to watch the sunset, vacuum the floor, reorganize drawers and cupboards, cook and practise yoga.

It was also a time to watch the news with horror and sadness, plus admiration and fascination. And of course, a time to learn how to operate Zoom, and the downside of backlighting!

I am old enough to remember a life with no technology. This experience would have been so very different without it. This pandemic gave technology an even more entrenched role in our lives, one that will have long-lasting effects.

So we have all, across the planet, learnt new things about life. From India to New Zealand, from Glasgow to Fowey, from Gambia to Alaska. Young and old, British, Native American, Croatian, Fijian, emigrating people, people who stay put – we are the generations who experienced the great COVID-19 pandemic, in myriad different ways.

It makes us special, and especially you, the people who will inherit the planet – the young. Finally, if it has changed anything, I hope it is that we have learnt to care more for each other and to be kind.

Helen

MARK RONSON
DJ and Record Producer

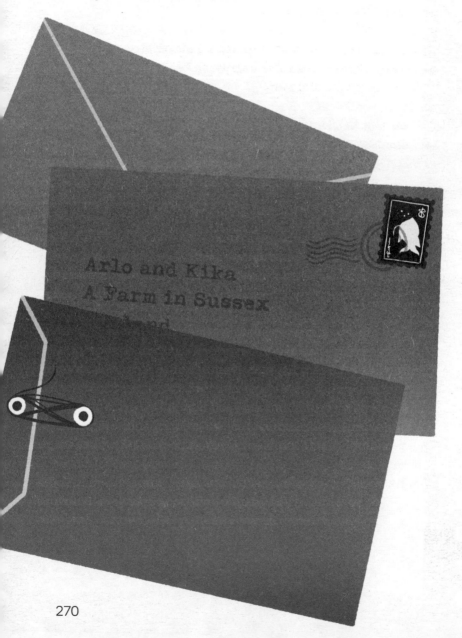

Arlo and Kika
A Farm in Sussex

Dear Arlo and Kika,

I was happy to receive your letter. You sound very lovely, and I'm happy to tell you a little about my Lockdown.

In the beginning, I really missed being around family and being in the studio, making music with all the people I love. But I got used to making some songs in my bedroom alone and taking some safe walks with my family. I also learnt to cook properly for the first time in my life - which was a lot of fun and sometimes a little disastrous!

Most importantly, it made me appreciate all the good things in life a lot and I hope to carry that with me even as the world starts to open back up.

I very much look forward to seeing this book you're putting together.

With love,

Mark Ronson

CHARLY COX
Poet. Writer.
Mental health activist

*Have someone read this to you and close your eyes. Hold
your own hand and imagine it's that of someone you love, or
someone you miss.*

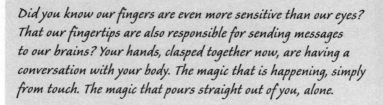

Dear Reader,

*Did you know our fingers are even more sensitive than our eyes?
That our fingertips are also responsible for sending messages
to our brains? Your hands, clasped together now, are having a
conversation with your body. The magic that is happening, simply
from touch. The magic that pours straight out of you, alone.*

*As your hands chatter away softly, whose hand is it that you are
imagining? Can you see their face as you think of their name?
Do you remember the colour of their eyes or the way they smell of
different washing powder to you? What is their mouth doing? Is it
smiling a big grin that's ready to let out a laugh or is it pursed and
small, ready to let you in on a secret?*

You can say anything you like to them and when their face or their eyes, their smell or their lips feel difficult to remember, squeeze your hand gently as though it is theirs and let your powerful fingertips bring them back. Let them stay with you, comfortable and safe, in your mind, in your hands.

How does your body feel holding the hand of the person you're imagining? Does it feel warm or calm? Does it feel excited or sad? Don't be frightened by them. Those feelings are there to remind you that the magic of the conversation between your hands is telling your body something: that person is with you. In your hands, in your imagination, in your heart.

It's been a pretty big year for hands, hasn't it? Hands have been washed, they've been sanitised, they've been dry and scratchy, and they've also saved lives. They've tapped on keyboards and painted rainbows. They've learnt so many incredible skills and shown us how capable we are of getting through hard things with how brilliantly they've held on to new routines and new ways. Now, they're ready to be there again, just for you. To hold hands with people you can see in person and those who you can't. Magic.

Charly Cox

273

LAST
LETTERS

MICHELE WALTER

Postwoman, Uckfield Delivery
Office, East Sussex

Dear Arlo and Kika,

I have been a post lady for 33 years and your post person for
eight of those. I have delivered thousands of letters during
that time but that's just a fraction of what Royal Mail deliver
– over 10 billion letters in the past year.

Because of the pandemic things have been quite different. My
day always starts very early in the morning when most people
are still asleep in bed. We have been extremely busy with
parcels and packets because the shops have been closed and
customers have chosen to order goods online instead.

We have to wear masks all the time we are in the office and
sort all the post in two waves so we can space ourselves out
more. That means that the first wave of people sort the
letters, parcels and packets whilst the others prepare their
rounds, then when the next lorry comes in, we swap over.
During normal times we would all be sorting together but
because of social distancing we have had to work differently.

Regarding friends – I am quite fortunate that I work with
most of mine and so see them almost every day. I am grateful
to have been working for a company that has been allowed to
keep going right through the pandemic. That said, I must

admit I was very apprehensive about going to work for the first couple of weeks when this all started. My customers all acted differently. Some kept to a normal distance, some wouldn't let you anywhere near them and some would get far too close, which I really didn't like. A number of my elderly customers were shielding. Parcels had to be left on the doorstep after you had rung the bell, stepped back and waited for them to answer.

I always really enjoy driving up to your farm to be met by a procession of fluffy barking dogs. Scribble, Doodle and Dot love to follow my van past your gates and if I'm lucky Molly, the 15-year-old grandmother, gives a final bark when I pull up.

Recently I have noticed some very interesting postmarks on your letters including 10 Downing Street, Buckingham Palace and some lovely stamps from all over the world. I am so excited to read some of the letters that I have been delivering to you in your book.

I have two daughters the same age as you. I hope they and all the other people who are reading this will start to write more letters. It is a lovely way of keeping in touch with your friends and family, far more personal than an email. Oh, and it keeps me busy which is a good thing.

Kindest regards,

Michele Walter

BUCKINGHAM PALACE

We even wrote to the Queen!

Dear Arlo and Kika,

The Queen has asked me to thank you for your letter, in which you told Her Majesty a little about your recent fundraising project.

Although The Queen is unable to respond personally, Her Majesty was pleased to hear from you and was touched that you should wish to share your thoughts and ideas with her.

The Queen hopes you, and your family, are keeping safe and well during the current situation, and I am to thank you, once again, for taking the time and trouble to write as you did.

Buckingham Palace

JAVED KHAN
Chief Executive of Barnardo's

Dear Arlo and Kika (and to all our wonderful readers),

First of all, congratulations on what you've achieved through this very special project.

You've managed to inspire some of the most famous people in the UK and around the globe to lend their support — from the world of politics, to the Royal Family, to Hollywood — which is highly impressive.

Most importantly, you've done a fantastic job at persuading so many people to share their experiences and to come together to support the charity Barnardo's, which exists to help some of the most vulnerable children and young people across the UK.

The Coronavirus pandemic has transformed all our lives. Many people have felt loss, anxiety and fear. I too have grieved for loved ones who have passed away because of COVID. And we've also missed some of the simple things in life that we used to take for granted — like handshakes, hugs, and sharing meals with loved ones.

The letters reflect the whole range of emotions we have experienced during this uniquely difficult time. What's particularly striking when reading the letters is the universal human experiences that unite people from such different backgrounds. The same themes occur again and again as people reflect on what matters most: family, friends, health, exercise, a connection with nature.

We know that young people have faced some of the toughest challenges since the pandemic began, especially during the Lockdowns. Many have had months away from teachers and friends, and it's not just the classes they've missed, but the sport, music and time in the playground.

As a society we know there are some things we used to do in person that work just as well online — but we also know school isn't one of them. And then of course there are the children who don't even have access to a laptop.

So it's hard to put into words exactly how much children and young people have struggled, and we can't know for sure what the longer term effects will be. But we do know that for some children, the legacy of COVID will live long after the virus is brought under control. Some children are grieving for loved ones, or are struggling with long-term anxiety. Some parents have lost their jobs or had their working hours reduced, meaning they are forced to decide between heating their homes, feeding their families or paying for data — essential for nearly all communications.

As a father, a former maths teacher, and now as the very fortunate Chief Executive of Barnardo's, I know that young people can achieve amazing things — even in the toughest of circumstances.

By creating this project, you have set a brilliant example to the rest of us. In reaching out to people from all walks of life, with all different jobs and backgrounds and interests, you have made us all feel connected.

Crucially, you have also brought people together for an important cause — to help Barnardo's to help the children and young people who are struggling most — now and in the months and years to come.

Barnardo's has been around for 155 years. The world has gone through huge transformations since then, but our purpose has remained the same. We bring care, support, hope and most importantly unconditional love, back into children's lives.

We know our vital services are needed more than ever before. We must continue helping families who are struggling, children suffering from mental health problems and young people at risk of harm.

But we can't do any of this without the generous support of lots of people — people like those reading this now.

At a time when so many of us have felt lonely or isolated, the letters in this book feel like hands of friendship reaching out to bring comfort and connection.

I think this is just what we need, as we prepare for a kinder, brighter, post-COVID world.

On behalf of everyone at the charity, I want say thank you to Arlo and Kika for putting their brilliant energy and enthusiasm to such a great cause; to our wonderful President Natasha for her generosity and determination in getting this published; to the team at Hachette for dedicating so much of their time; and of course to all the incredible people who have shared their lockdown experiences.

Finally, I want to thank you, the reader, for buying this book and helping us to support the children and young people who need us most.

Javed Khan

ACKNOWLEDGEMENTS

I love saying thank you – and there are so many to thank.

The first and most important thanks, is, of course, to the children and young adults supported by Barnardo's who have inspired so many extraordinary letter writers to contribute to this anthology. If you are one of these people, and Barnardo's is part of your life, thank you. Everyone who has contributed to this book has done so knowing that you are our future, and that we believe in you and the contribution you will make to society as your life progresses. Young people have paid a high price to keep us all safe during the pandemic, and now we must put your futures first. We wish you the best of luck as you make big life choices – and hope that as you do so, you feel the support and love that surrounds you.

To all the Barnardo's staff who operate the over 800 services we provide, and who have the privilege of working with such special young people, thank you for your dedication and selflessness. The challenges that face society are great, but they would be insurmountable without your commitment. Please know that you have my endless admiration and respect.

And now for the rest . . .

Thank you to my brother Ben, who has the very good fortune to be friends with David Shelley, CEO of Hachette UK, who linked me to the wonderful team who supported this project when publishing a collection of 'Letters From Lockdown' was a random idea in the middle of the night. Hilary Murray Hill, Ruth Alltimes, Emily Thomas, Beth McWilliams, Helen Hughes, Laura Pritchard, and the sales teams didn't take much persuading to throw their weight behind this project and have facilitated the three-month turnaround of this book.

Special thanks are reserved for Tig Wallace, our brilliant editor, who has expertly guided us to publication through endless Zooms from his front room to ours. Samantha Romp has been an invaluable support – without her tech expertise, I fear Arlo and Kika would have been the only beneficiaries from the humour, wisdom, and advice of the proceeding correspondence. Samuel Perrett has made all these letters look so beautiful while working to the incredibly tight last-minute deadlines this book demanded.

I am, of course, endlessly grateful to our wonderful family, friends, and colleagues from all over the world who so generously opened their address books to connect us to the extraordinary range of contributors in this book.

To our wonderful contributors – thank you so very much for sharing your Lockdown experiences. There is no doubt you will have inspired many through your carefully selected words. Hopefully, together we will have captured something of the private journeys we have all been on and helped to create some form of emotional time capsule documenting a little of what we all did behind closed doors throughout the pandemic.

Thank you to Justin, Arlo and Kika's amazing father, who has provided endless support on so many levels, and who, on more than one occasion, has patiently plucked glitter stars out of the printer (with only the occasional complaint!) The best bit about Lockdown has been the chance to spend so much time with you. Thank you.

My last thanks are to the four-legged support team who have seen Tig, Sam and me through endless Zoom meetings as we have weaved these letters together. To Molly, my faithful loyal companion of 15 years; to Rascal, who has beautifully adorned the background of Tig's Zoom squares and to the newest member of the team, Sam's Otto, who has added a little frisson to meetings on account of his penchant for electrical cables.

Thank you to you all.

Stay safe and positive. One of these days,
all of this will just be a memory.

Natasha xx

WHAT NEXT?

After reading these letters, we hope you might feel inspired to write one too.

Maybe to someone you haven't seen in a while, or to an elderly relative, or to a friend abroad.

We know you'll enjoy picking up a pen and writing, almost as much as someone will enjoy reading your letter!